"Ordinary" Children, Extraordinary Teachers

MARVA COLLINS

"Ordinary" Children, Extraordinary Teachers

HAMPTON ROADS
PUBLISHING COMPANY, INC.

Hampton Roads Publishing Company, Inc.
134 Burgess Lane
Charlottesville, VA 22902
Or call: (804) 296-2772
FAX: (804) 296-5096

If you are unable to order this book from your local
bookseller, you may order directly from the publisher.
Call 1-800-766-8009, toll-free.

Cover design by Patrick Smith

ISBN 1-878901-41-9

10 9 8

Printed in Canada

Contents

PART III.
Inspiration For Us All

Introduction

When I first wrote *Marva Collins' Way* several years ago, I thought that education was as bad as it could get. However, the last eight years have presented me with many experiences to see schools all across America, and I have found that what I once assumed to be inferior education for the poor has also become the malady of the middle and upper classes. I have found bad education in the places I least expected to find it. Teachers are not bad; they are doing what they learned to do. They learned from professors in college who have never taught school a day in their lives. Parents do care about their children. Few parents actually want to claim an illiterate as their child. No principals or superintendents want to have it said that they have bad school systems. However, educators have unknowingly become mired in a system that, unfortunately, fails more children than it helps. Unsuspecting parents, teachers, and administrators are working as hard as they know how to work with materials that, unfortunately, decimate more children than they help, and so, once again, young teachers just entering the teaching profession haven't the slightest idea of what makes for a good academic program. Children, therefore, can actually get through school checking true and false answers and guessing at multiple choice questions that they never learned to read.

Just one example of bad education is how we teach young children to read. For example, when we begin teaching reading, the average American child learns that "a" is symbolic of unlocking words such as "apple," "at," etc., but we are missing seven other spellings for "a," and they are:

"eight," "aigh," "a-e," "ay," "ea," "eigh," "ey," and "ai." Our three and four-year-olds are taught every spelling there is for unlocking any "a" word, and they become lifetime readers rather than "Workbook idiots."

To give us some idea as to how bad the schools are, let us look at a few quotes from several corporate people:

In a *Wall Street Journal* article, Joseph F. Alibrandi, chief executive of Whittaker Corporation, states, "The public schools don't work worth a damn. Band-Aids won't work any more. We need a total restructuring of the public schools."

Thomas Donahoe, president of the Pacific Telesis Group's company foundation, states, "Unless there are fundamental reforms going on, we are convinced there will be little long term good."

Robert C. Winters, chairman of the Prudential Insurance Company, stated in a speech delivered at Princeton University, "It is time to stop blaming the children. . .last year 44 percent of all those who applied for work at our Newark office. . .were unable to read at the 9th-grade level. They are 17 years old and virtually unemployable for life. The time has come for systematic. . .educational reform. In fact, what we really need is not just reform, but a revolution."

"Chicago's public schools are the worst in the nation," said William Bennett, former Secretary of Education.

We hear a lot about school reform today, and I feel that it is irresponsible to turn our worst schools over to our struggling communities and expect that, by some magic, inner-city schools will improve. We need much higher levels of parental involvement. We need principals who are strong and respected and who care more about the students than they do about personality polls. We need skilled, dedicated, highly-respected, and well-compensated new teachers in our teaching force. In order to meet these needs system-wide, we need skilled and paid new leadership working full time at the top and committed citizens working in volunteer capacities at each school. The success of any enterprise depends on the quality of the people in it.

The chapters in this book are no panacea for the maladies of our time. Our methodology is nothing less than the basic three R's mixed with a total program that teaches every child that he is unique, special, and bright and that we will not let him *fail.*

We have no monopoly on excellence at Westside Preparatory School; we simply do not buy into the idea that "poor inner-city children cannot achieve." We expect universal standards from our children, and no teacher here will accept anything less than that. We do manage to teach our boys and girls here to write, read, compute, and to think critically and analytically.

We provide an academic ambience in everything that we do here at Westside Preparatory School. Each Friday is set aside as our Mentally Gifted Forum (MGM Forum) where six-, seven-, and eight- year-olds lecture to all of the students in the school. Each student must research, write, and memorize his lecture. No notes are allowed. The audience must make notes of the lectures and ask questions at the end of the lectures.

Each weekend finds the group here assembled to partake in debates, spelling contests, vocabulary contests, math relays, science relays, etc.

Each child must also compile a list of the qualities of a giant. Those qualities are then hung in each classroom, and when a child recidivates, he is asked to go back and look at the list that he has compiled to pick the quality that he is not exhibiting at this time. In other words, discipline and academic excellence are self-administered. I find that most schools attempt the school year without having well-defined goals for what they expect for each student.

All students at Westside Preparatory School must also take an oral pledge before the entire group that they will never bring disgrace to the school and that they will, at all times, uphold the moral and academic standards of Westside Preparatory School and that any student who is guilty of omission in this area does not deserve the right to be called a Westside Prepian. The academic program at Westside

Preparatory is nothing less than the basic three R's mixed with a total program that teaches all children that they are unique, special, and that they are too bright to ever be less than all that they can be. The "I will not let you fail" statement is one that they seldom hear elsewhere. We also hold parent classes, and we teach the very same things to parents that we teach our students.

As I listened today to three- and four-year-olds reading about Daedalus and Icarus, one four-year-old declared: "Mrs. Collins, if we do not learn and work hard, we will take an Icarian flight to nowhere." I somehow wished that the whole world could see and understand that all children are born achievers and all they need is someone to help them become all that they have the potential to become.

To me, it is so easy to declare what students cannot do, but I always tell the teachers who work here that a good teacher will always make the "poor" student good and the "good" student superior. The word *teacher* is a Latin word meaning "to lead or to draw out." The good teacher is always willing to polish and shine until the true shining lustre of each student shines through.

School, in my opinion, should be a miniature society where students can practice to become good citizens in the real world. It seems, however, that we as educators work anathema to that goal today. I often wonder why so many teachers hand papers back to students with the statement that says, "Incomplete sentences; do over." Judas Priest! If the student knew what to do he would have done it correctly in the first place.

It must also seem very strange to students that many, many teachers allow them to speak in incomplete sentences, and yet they are supposed to write in complete sentences. When any teacher at Westside Preparatory School inquires as to how a student is each morning, the student is never allowed to respond in a one word statement such as "Okay" or "Fine"; instead, he must reply, "Good morning, Miss Jones. I am fine, thank you. And you?" When students are completing a math problem or a writing assignment, a teacher is always there to mediate errors before they become permanent ones red-marked with negative comments.

Likewise, we never have students write mundane lines such as "I will not chew gum in class." They must write a paper on the etymology of *gum,* or perhaps a paper titled "I Am Too Bright to Waste My Time Chewing Gum in School," etc.

Since our society depends on the morals of its citizens, I am always amazed at the banalities of the content taught students. When a child reads, "See Sue. See Sue run. Run, Sue, run," I often wonder what moral conclusion he ends up with. Meanwhile, our children begin reading *Aesop's Fables,* and every story throughout our curriculum has a moral tone. Selections such as the *Pied Piper of Hamelin, Androcles and the Lion, Pilgrim's Progress,* and others teach students the morals of stick-to-itiveness, determination, perseverance, etc. We must never forget the lessons inherent in Gibbon's *Rise and Fall of the Roman Empire.* Once all roads led to Rome. Rome was considered the greatest empire ever. That good-enough attitude, however, meant that the Romans felt that good meant forever, and they also became an amoral society, and any society without morals is bound to crumble. Socrates was right when he said, "Straight thinking leads to right living." Just as we are what we eat, likewise, we too are what we learn.

To take students from many inner-city backgrounds, or any other background, and attempt to teach without explaining what's in it for them is pretty much like putting a Band-Aid on a hemorrhage. Students must first be taught to like themselves, and each day must serve as a convincing factor of the things that they can do "right." Few of us can sustain a relationship in which everything we do is wrong and we are always told what is wrong with us. This is why we never say to a student, "This is wrong." We always say, "Good try, but let's proofread this or that." The word "proofread," to me, sounds better than the word "wrong."

I.
"Ordinary" Children

1

Children Do Not Fail

I started Westside Prep in the fall of 1975 because I felt there were far too many children being recruited for failure, far too many excuses being used for not educating children. I live on the west side of Chicago, near where our school is located, and somehow I felt there were too many lives just hanging out there in a perilous vacuum, so I decided to start my own school. Using $5,000 from my pension fund (I had been teaching in public schools for 14 years), we knocked down a wall between two rooms in the upstairs of our house and bought some desks; my husband installed some panelling, and Westside Prep opened its doors on September 8, 1975.

For the first four years we continued to meet in that upstairs schoolroom, cramming 34 desks side by side, using every conceivable inch. We took children who had been expelled from our public schools, who had dropped out in discouragement, or who were simply failing, or being labeled as incorrigible and unteachable. All of the students proceeded to learn and many have now gone on to the best high schools and colleges available. There were no miracles. There is nothing miraculous or magical about their successes. It took only love and determination.

My own philosophy has always been to make the poor student good and the good student superior, with no excuses in between. That has always been my belief, and that is pretty much what we practice at Westside Prep. I also think it's important not to spend so much time being an adult that we forget what it is like to be a child. In every problem situation that children get into, I usually ask myself, "How would I have felt at that age?" I always try to remember what I did as a student in school. I was not perfect, so how can I expect my children to be perfect? We often forget that we've done the very same things as the children.

We also tend to lose perspective; we fail to understand that children have only known us as adults. They assume we were born adults. I think that's the strange thing adults do not realize, because we have been adults as long as they've known us. I think we have to let them know that we did pretty much the same things when we were children, and to somehow let them know that "once when I was a child I did such and such. . ." which puts them at ease and takes away the image of a demi-god that teachers, unfortunately, sometimes have in the eyes of children.

Basics, with Positive Reinforcement

On the kind of budget we have, and with our philosophy, we do not need what might be called "teaching frills"—things like film projectors, teaching machines, calculators for the children, and the like. We deal in basics.

I tell my teachers that the four-year-olds who start with us in September must be reading by Christmas—no ifs, ands, or buts, no excuses, no in-betweens. I don't want to hear why they can't, what they don't know, what the problems with them are. I tell the teachers they are responsible for making them learn, and they have to work hard to see that the children succeed; otherwise the teachers will have to be replaced.

At all levels, the teacher can never write anything negative about a child, such as, "He doesn't work up to his potential" or "He doesn't sit still." Everything is positive. I tell the teachers that if a student does not sit still, the teacher is responsible for finding out why. Maybe the "oven is too hot," and we need to make it more comfortable. Or, maybe we need to look at the way the teacher is presenting something. We will not accept failure; there is always a reason why a student is not succeeding.

The teacher sets the ambience in any classroom. The teacher has total control over the learning environment and children respond exactly to the atmosphere a teacher creates. Teachers have been known to ridicule children, or to laugh if a child cannot get the answer, even subtly. Nothing could be worse for a child. In our school the teacher and the rest of the children pull for a child to get it right. You can just see them mentally pulling for the child. And then, when he finally gets the right answer, or finally syllabicates the word correctly, you get this long applause from every child. It's like a total family, and it starts with the teacher, setting the climate for support and care.

Our approach postures the children as the big *YOUs,* and the teacher as the little *I.* Everything is for the children. We find something positive to say about a child every morning. For example, the kids will pass by my room and I'll say, "I like your gym shoes. I like your ribbon. I like your barrette. I like your shirt. I like your blue jeans." We find something to say that is complimentary to every child. This is just as important as a curriculum.

As I go across the country, I have occasion to visit a great many schools and invariably the good teacher is in there teaching; the poor teacher is in there giving excuses. The good teacher invariably has an exciting classroom where children are learning—the same kind of ambience we have in our classrooms. The poor teachers all across the country are in screaming and yelling, and as they scream, the students often scream back, and a lot of children simply turn off. I find it to be a universal situation: there are good teachers everywhere, there are poor teachers everywhere. The good ones are constantly trying to find answers, the poor ones are constantly making excuses.

In the last year we have had about 2,500 visitors in our school, and the good teachers come in and sit with me all day and they say, "Oh, this is how you do what you do." The poor teachers, on the other hand, are busy stealing our papers from the wall because they think by osmosis they can grab a paper from the wall and go back to their school and do what we do. They miss the whole point of what real teaching is.

Universality of Children's Needs

Maybe there's something wrong with me, but I don't think in terms of "red, green, black, white, pink, pinstripe, polka-dot, etc." I think quality and I think universality. If I encounter prejudice or a situation that could become prejudicial, I say to our children, "That's that person's problem. Don't become part of the problem too. You have to be bigger than the problem because the smartest man won't insult you, no fool can."

I believe this type of attitude helps our students avoid arguing with each other about trivial things. For example, I will say to two children who are arguing about a pencil, "Why not spend those energies and time trying to figure out how to own the entire pencil company, rather than wanting to knock someone's head off about one single pencil." And as they think about it, it makes a lot of sense to them.

This way of looking at things, so that a small incident is seen as part of a larger picture, is important and takes place inside and outside of the classroom. Some of my most important work with children takes place at lunchtime. I have always insisted on eating lunch with my children instead of being separated off with the other teachers. I try to rotate, sitting next to a different child every day. A particular child might come to school without lunch; some children have problems all the way around. A student's situation is often consistent; no lunch money, no skills, no self-image either. These students will tell me they are not hungry, and I tell them if they won't eat, I'm not going to eat either. Eventually we share, and the children come to learn that we are all in this together.

Then when the other children see me accepting the child, they learn to accept that child too. Everyone wants to be accepted by the teacher and students know that in order to gain acceptance, they must accept a rejected child. As a teacher, you have to be accepting of everyone—the child who's fat, the child who's homely, the child who suffers for whatever reasons. You say to the other children, by your actions, that you are accepting that child and you expect the rest of the children to accept him, too. It does not and cannot be in a verbal way, because you cannot force children to be accepting. But by saying to that runny-nosed child, "You're such a handsome boy. I love you" (and they look back at you as if to say, "Who, me? I can't believe it!"), you are providing a model of behavior for all children to follow.

Social acceptance at school is very important, and we as adults forget how difficult it is for a new child. If I see a child standing on the sidelines, I go outside and join the gang. I never tell the children to let him play because then you put him in a bad situation. I simply take his hand and join another child's hand and he becomes part of a circle and I do that until he is accepted. Then I assign a couple of partners to the new student (and usually I assign the problem students—the children who might sock him in the bathroom when I'm not looking). I don't think teachers realize that when a child is new in school, he is self-conscious and frustrated and wants more than anything to be accepted.

The Total Child

We emphasize a total learning experience. Not only must students be able to pass tests, perform academically, and work through social situations, but they must also have a sense of humanity and compassion. To be bright and not have feelings can lead to incredible inhumanity. I think we must remember what happened in Auschwitz. Here were people who were very, very bright, but they used their intelligence in an attempt to destroy an entire race. They lost a sense of feeling, and their brightness became an inhumanity to man.

I'll often say to my students that we can be ever so clever, but we also have to learn first how to be human. That's why I emphasize philosophy as found in some of the world's classic literary works. The students study Ralph Emerson's *Self-Reliance* and can quote the famous line, "Any man who would be a man must be a non-conformist." I think that's very important, for among other things, it helps develop individuality and a respect for differences.

Everything a teacher does affects children. That's why you, as a teacher, must be aware of what resources are available, and you must know the moralities of what children read, the actual lessons of life you want them to take into the world. Perhaps this can help explain the reaction our students create in the eyes of objective observers. Many of the visitors who come into our school say our children are so different. They are surprised our children do not act as if they detest whites or do not seem to have the racial hatred that many children have. I think this is because, as Socrates said, "Once a man can be made to be shown good, he will always choose it." These children are so busy learning, they have been shown what is good and what it means to succeed, that they don't have time for racial hatred and petty bigotry.

Once students catch the spirit of learning, they have learned how to tick, how to make the most of what they are. Then they learn how to tick better. They do not have time to worry about what color people may be because they feel good about themselves. Tensions between races or between countries stem from a lack of understanding and an abundance of misunderstanding between cultures. Simply put, an educated population can help solve problems among people and ultimately help us in our goal of world peace. This is, perhaps, the most important and least acknowledged goal of education.

Social Problems and Education

Many of the social problems afflicting our country stem from a lack of good teaching and the failure of our schools to provide a solid education. We have more crime than ever, we have alcohol problems, drug abuse, and a suicide rate among children and teenagers that is epidemic—all because many children never really discover their unique selves. They never really discover that what they are seeking is already within them, like the characters from *The Wizard of Oz,* each of whom already had what he was looking for. The Lion already had courage, the Tin Man already had a heart.

We seek this and we seek that, but maybe it is already within our realms, and if we stop looking outside ourselves and look inside, deeply and intelligently, it is probably there waiting for us.

Education is the one crucial thing that is accessible to all, and without it a man can become like a wild beast. That does not mean that people with degrees are educated. That might be a "surface education." I think we need to know a lot about a lot of things—the essence of a true liberal arts education—in order to make exceptions. How else can we know what we really don't like?

There are people who say they do not like Polish people, for instance, and I ask them if they have met all the Polish people in the world. Of course they haven't. How can one intelligently decide what one likes or dislikes unless one knows all there is to know? That is why syllogistic reasoning is so important, and unfortunately, we have just about eliminated it in most of our schools. We have gotten away from any kind of deep thinking in our teaching, yet perceptive, intelligent, sensitive responses are so crucial to world peace, not to mention within our own communities.

Welcome to Success

When I teach any class, I usually detect a child who wants to act out, and often it is the older boy in the back of the room who is clowning around. I stand right behind that child with my hand on his shoulder and talk directly to him because the children who are behaving do not need my attention. The tendency many teachers have is to ignore these children—they're usually in the back of the room and they usually see themselves as failures. Sometimes I will actually do their work for them, just to give them a taste of success.

I helped one lad with his papers for the first two weeks. I literally went by his desk every day and did his work for him. His response was, "Wait until my old lady see this!" He said "old lady" the first time. Of course, it was "my mother" after a month. He said he had never gotten 100 on a paper in his life. One night his mother called and accused me of helping him with his paper because, as she said, "He always fails everything. He could never have done so well on his own." I told her that failure was what he didn't need any more of. He already knows how to fail; he is in school to learn how to succeed.

When our children walk in the door, I say, "Welcome to success. Say goodbye to failure because you are not going to fail. I'm not going to let you fail. You are here to win, you were born to win and if I have to care more about you than you care about you, that's the way it will be." It doesn't matter what kind of disciplinary problems they had in previous schools; they are with us to succeed. We will not let them fail.

Many of our students are from the inner city. Most have been problems for either their parents or their schools, usually both. The male student, the inner city black male, is a real problem for some schools or school districts. Teachers often seem fearful of these boys, but they don't realize these children have something wonderful and special inside that is trying to escape. They remind me of what Michelangelo said about a piece of marble: "Inside is an angel trying to get out." I think of that in our school environment. There is a great deal of toughness and tough talk on the street and in the school but inside is a child who wants to be accepted, a child who wants to succeed.

The violence that all too often erupts in our schools (and in our society) is just a sign that there is pressure on the child, and he is begging for someone to relieve him of that pressure. I think once he finds a way to succeed, he will be relieved of acting out that violence, and he will be at peace within himself. In our school, the children do not give a "problem child" an audience. Therefore, there is no need for him to act out, there is no laughing if he gets smart-alecky or if he comes out with a comment. Everyone continues working as if he said the most normal thing in the world. The pressure is relieved; there is no longer an audience or a need to act out.

Positive Discipline

One of my goals is to turn disciplinary situations into positive lessons. For example, if I have a child who likes to draw in my classroom, instead of telling him to stop the doodling, I tell him what a beautiful picture he has made and ask him to write a story about it. So, he is not only drawing without fear of reprisal, he is also getting the writing skills I want him to acquire.

I think you have to react positively to whatever children do. If they are acting up or chewing gum, I have them write a composition on the "Art of Blowing Bubbles" in which they write about the ingredients, the first gum ever made, the etymology of the word *gum,* and so forth. I grade that paper as if it were a regular assignment and make sure that it gets a prominent place on the hallway wall. Then the older children will say to the new children coming in, "You don't ever want to chew gum in here because by the time you finish writing your gum essay, complete with an outline and bibliography, you'll never want to see a piece of gum again." Whatever happens, the teacher can and really must make it into a learning situation.

If a child shoots a rubber band, right away some teachers are busy writing a report saying all kinds of negative things about the child rather than just taking the rubber band away. This only exacerbates the problem. I never miss a beat. The other day, a child had a pair of karate sticks. I just went by the desk and said "give me those." I put them in my purse and that was the end of it. I did not go into a long dialogue or send the student to the office or issue a punishment or embarrass the student. Again, I think we forget what it is like to be a child. I think we tend to make too much out of nothing.

Acting Out is a Signal

Teachers never bother to ask children if there is a problem in the home. Too often, this leaves the teacher unaware of the child's needs. Perhaps the mother or father has deserted the child, perhaps a divorce or separation is in the works, or perhaps some other emotional problem is at hand. Usually, when children act out, or when children refuse to learn, it is a signal that something is wrong, just as an illness or pain is a signal that something is physically wrong with us.

I do not think educators see this as a signal. It sometimes helps to take a child aside, put your hand on his shoulders and say, "Now we all hurt. I have problems too and we all hurt inside. You can tell me about it." When children know that you care, they even begin to tell you things that they often do not communicate to their parents. Too often, we try to put Band-Aids on hemorrhages. Spending more money on creating new programs usually doesn't help. Human care, human concern, is the only way to help these situations.

When a child has skills, when he feels good about himself, he has no reason to hurt other people; he has no reason to act out. And any child, be he black, white, green, or whatever, is going to act out when something hurts. Either the teacher or the parent is responsible and I always feel that I work against the odds. I consider myself parent and teacher. It is my responsibility to let my lessons go for a few minutes to find out what may be bothering this child. I try to empathize with whatever is bothering him, in hopes of making him feel he is not alone. Once I find out what the problem is, together we find a way to deal with it.

Phonics Approach to Reading

We give all of our students daily exercises in phonics. I am convinced it is the most effective way to teach reading and I'm sure this is the reason our students are able to read Shakespeare, Thoreau, Emerson, Tolstoy, and many other classical authors.

The phonics approach to teaching reading has been articulated and explained in many sources, most recently in Rudolph Flesch's *Why Johnny Still Can't Read*. Flesch does a good job of countering the look-and-say method which, for some reason, gained enormous popularity in this country over the last twenty or so years, continuing up through today. Look-and-say has, in fact, done more to keep children from becoming good readers than anything else. Briefly, the look-and-say method has children look at a word, for example, "look," and then has them pronounce the word. There is no context; it is merely a word which the child reads and then pronounces. He learns to look at it configuratively, by the way it looks. But when the child sees the word in another context, in a sentence, or out of context, he often does not recognize the same word.

With the phonetic method, children actually learn to sound out the vowels and all of the other sounds. There are about 93 basic sounds in the English language. With phonics, you simply learn every sound, every syllable, and most of the spoken words in the English language. In this approach, the children are first taught the letters of the alphabet and then they learn the sounds of each letter in the alphabet. This ensures every teacher that the children will not only learn to read selected materials, but will learn how to read for a lifetime. We teach children not only to read, but also to learn to read for a lifetime.

For example, as I go across the country doing consulting work, I notice that most teachers teach children that the sound of "a" has the sound of "a" as in "bat," and they wait until the child is in second or third grade to teach the long vowels; I believe that if children are taught all the sounds simultaneously, they then can better differentiate between the sounds. Eg., the sounds for A are: "a-e" read "a blank e," "eigh" as in "eight," "aigh" as in "straight," the schwa sound as in "America" which says the sound "uh," "ey" that says "long a" as in "they," and "-ay" as in "play." The children are taught to say the sound as "blank ay says a as in play, day, relay"; "ea says long a as in steak, break," "ai says long a as in sail, fail, jail." In other words, children learn to read, write and spell simultaneously. This means that we do not pull another book to teach spelling and handwriting. It makes more sense to me to teach children to read, write, spell, and learn all the spellings for "a" at the same time rather than saying a year or so later, "By the way, children, 'a' also says whatever." The teaching of long and short vowels together ensures that children can better differentiate between the sounds. Most readers teach children only the short vowels in first grade, and the average page in the average basal reader treats children like "idiots." The pages contain only the short vowels and a repetition of words that encourages memory work rather than reading.

I have found that the other teachers are just as addicted to teaching as I am, but it's not just an addiction to teaching; it's an addiction to learning. The teachers tell me they never knew there was so much to learn, and they never realized teaching could be so fascinating. We have created an attitude that puts joy back into learning. That creates satisfaction at doing something correctly.

Our approach pushes students to excel, and students like to be pushed. They want to do well. They want to succeed. And once they have a taste of it, they will never again settle for mediocrity. We *are not dealing in miracles, we are dealing in oneself.*

Once you, as a teacher, experience the excitement of seeing children standing up and clapping when you finish reading Leo Tolstoy's "Where God Is, Love Is," for example, and see them coming closer and closer to where you are standing, you realize you have them doing what you want them to do: learning and being excited about the adventure of new ideas.

Basically, all that teachers need to do is to admit they do not know. I do not think anything can be changed until a teacher admits that he or she has a great deal left to learn. Once this realization is reached, those who are interested in the joy of learning and teaching, and in seeing the joy in children's faces, do not want to go home at the end of the day. Instead, they wonder where the day went. As teachers, we are never in the land of "done." We are always in the land of "doing."

Some teachers think that just what is given to them in the classroom is all there is to be used. These are very poor teachers. You have to go beyond. A child living and staying in the same neighborhood all of his life will never realize there is a wider world out there. The same thing applies to teachers. To just read what is given to me in a classroom and not explore other means and not explore other connecting topics, still guarantees failure as a teacher.

Learning is everywhere. I think that is the one thing that is missing in the minds of many teachers. Everything in life has knowledge attached to it, and students are just waiting to learn things. But it is not to be found just within the four walls of the classroom, or in the teacher's guide. Your mind has to take it a bit farther, you have to run that extra mile sometimes, but the knowledge is there, and the attitude is there, and the good teacher will take the time to look and dig until it is found. Once you have it, there is no stopping you and I promise that your students will catch the same exciting spirit of learning.

2.
Relighting the Candles of Excellence in America

When I was growing up in Alabama, my mother often warned me that my determination would get me into something one day that I would never get out of. And I am often reminded of that when I see that my present schedule now runs three to four years ahead with lecture bookings. Somehow, Westside Preparatory School seems to have become almost a clearing house for problem areas all over the country. Just a day before I came here, the Bush Transition Team asked if I would once again consider becoming Secretary of Education. As if I didn't have enough to battle with already. How many presidents do you keep saying No to? I had to say No to the Reagan Administration when they asked me the very same question. Of course, the real question is: where can I make the greatest contribution, teaching the most children with the most freedom?

We call the kind of education that we give at Westside Preparatory School, "free education." Not free in the fact that it is free monetarily. We're forever struggling financially because I refuse all federal funds. We have no corporate grants. The only outside funding at Westside Preparatory School is the money I receive from my lectures and from training teachers who come to us from all over the world to be trained. In the last two years, I have trained 4,700 teachers, principals, and administrators from all over the world.

What I'd like to say to those of you who are educators, who are parents, and who are young students going into teaching, is that I think we have forgotten the inherent principles, the basic principles, the foundations, the morals, the ethics that made this a great country. It was certainly dedication, commitment, and people caring. Often, when hearing young people say, "I do not want to go into teaching because it does not pay enough," I think of all the wonderful rewards that they will never know. I turned down a million dollars just last year to start 100 Marva Collins, Inc., schools across the country—I knew that I could not live with myself if there was one child in one of those schools not learning. And I thought that it would become much too much of a Herculean task to staff 100 schools across the country with teachers—with dedicated teachers, motivated teachers, and teachers who teach because they care.

We can all pay teachers to teach, but how much do you really pay a teacher to care? I have been very fortunate to have a very bright, energetic, dedicated staff who all take personally the failure of just one child. We all have the attitude that just one more time, one more attempt with the child would somehow help us save that child. And I'm very proud to say that Calvin College is the first U.S. college which started to send its students of education to Westside Preparatory to be trained. We have a new group of students from Calvin College who come here this January. Other colleges across the United States also send their students to us, but Calvin College was the very first.

And I think the critique forms that those students sent back to their professors say that they found an inner-city school works because of motivated leadership and dedication from the teachers. And they found that a lot of preconceived ideas about what inner-city children could, or could not, learn, changed.

We all hear the doomsday cries about where education is today and how decadent our schools are. The government admits we now have 23 million illiterates and 35 million functional illiterates, with two million illiterates being added to that figure each year. We have been called A Nation At Risk. If that does not frighten you, it certainly frightens me. Thomas Jefferson told us 200 years ago that we cannot be a powerful nation and illiterate too. I think some of us have become either comfortable or anesthetized to all of the doomsday cries, all the bad press, the bad things that happen today. And I think we've begun historically what has happened to empires, cities, states, countries, who thought that they could rest from their past morals and thought that *good* meant *forever*. We must never forget the lessons of the rise and fall of the Roman Empire: They once too thought they were good and that *good* meant *forever*.

We have many problems in this country, but if we visit other countries, we see it is still the greatest country on earth. And each of us here today shares certain inalienable freedoms and privileges given us by people who did not ask what was in it for them. I think that it is fine to be literate and to be bright, but just being bright is not enough. We let our students know it is their responsibility to give something back to the world. As soon as our children are old enough, they must sign a contract, as to what their contributions will be to the world. We would say to our 7-year-olds, "How old are you now?" "I'm seven." "How old will you be 10 years from now?" "I will be seventeen." "What do you intend to be doing when you're seventeen, and what are you doing about it now?"

Just being bright is not enough. We certainly know what happened with brilliance in Auschwitz. They were very brilliant. But they used that brilliance to destroy humanity. We have to get some morality back into our classrooms. The entire curriculum that I devised for Westside Preparatory School begins with a creed that every child memorizes, and some of the lines from that creed state, "Life is not served to me on a proverbial platter. I will discourage being average."

Every child at Westside Preparatory knows that average professionals are never in short supply. The world is looking for people, for students, for citizens who are above average. Our children realize that if they do not work, they do not eat. There is not one child in our school that will not tell you that. Our three- and four-year-olds are reading at the first-grade level. By Christmas, the first story they learn to read is "The

Little Red Hen." And of course, the lesson inherent there is that, "If I do not work, I do not eat." The Little Red Hen found that everybody wanted to help her eat the bread, but nobody wanted to help her plant it, take it to the mill, or do any of the work.

At Westside Preparatory, we begin to teach our children with heaping doses of phonics. As I go across the country, I am appalled at how children are attempting to learn to read with a method that was devised by Gallaudet, who started the first teacher's college for the deaf. And then when Horace Mann started teacher colleges he said, "Well, if this method works so well with deaf children, surely it must do wonders with normal children." We use a method in America to teach our children today that was devised to teach deaf mutes. And that's still one of the mysteries of Western Civilization, as to why we continue to use this method. We teach children that A is symbolic of apple, but what about "eigh" instead of "a," or "ea" which says "a" sometimes, as in "steak" and "break"? What we do is teach children every spelling for the "a" sound that there will ever be.

When the educators who come into our school complete their critique forms at the end of their sessions, they all say our expectations for students are very high. If we allowed children to use incomplete sentences in our classes, and then we write on their papers "incomplete sentences," well, Judas Priest! We've allowed them to speak in incomplete sentences, so they don't know what writing complete sentences is all about. When we say to a student, "Good morning, How are you?" they can never just retort, "Fine, O.K." They must answer in a complete sentence, "I am fine, thank you, Mrs. Brown." "I am fine, thank you, Mrs. Collins."

Some teachers give children their papers to do over again. If the children knew what to do, they would have done them correctly the very first time. None of our teachers has a desk. Every teacher walks from student to student to mediate errors before they become permanent errors. Teachers in some schools tell a child in the back row, "If you have a problem, raise your hand." Well, usually students do not know when they have a problem. The word "teacher" is a Latin word, meaning "to lead or to draw out." Our teachers are there at every moment to make certain those errors do not become permanent ones. If you red-mark papers and give them back to students a week, two weeks later, the errors mean very little to them. Usually, those papers end up in the nearest garbage pail.

At Westside Preparatory, we are there at that moment to say to them (We always find something positive to say about their papers), "Very good, but let's proofread this."

No teacher ever uses the words, "That's wrong." We wonder why students hate school so terribly today, but none of us likes to go places—work places or classrooms—where we hear, "That's wrong"! Whatever our professions, we want to be told something that's good about us. We always find something positive to say about a child.

If we ask an oral question, we use a lot of the Socratic Method: teacher-pupil dialogue. We are not much for the Xerox sheets where children only have to check "T" for true or "F" for false, or guess at multiple-choice questions. There is a dialogue between the teacher and pupil every day. Our blackboards are perhaps the most utilized tool in our classrooms. We believe that when a child is developing a mathematical problem at the blackboard, we are there to show him where he's going wrong, rather than trying to have him maybe complete 10 or 12 problems erroneously. We feel that it is better to correct those errors immediately. As soon as our children learn to read, they must read one classic every two weeks and report it to us orally. That means every teacher in our school must also have read that book. What happens with written book reports, is that they will either use Cliff Notes or they will write the beginning of the book, the middle, and the end.

Children have an uncanny way of being very creative. I remember once when I was still teaching in the classroom, a young lady stood up to read a poem that she had written. And I said, "That's very good, Erica. Did you really write that?" She said, "I really did, Mrs. Collins." I said, "Gee, that's wonderful. That's superlative, but did you really do that?" She said, "I did." And I kept trying to get her to tell the truth that she didn't. So I finally said, "That's very good, Erica, but that came from page 32 of the March issue of *Cricket* magazine. And you could hear the entire class just go, "Oooooo," and finally one lad said, "Don't you know you can't fool Mrs. Collins?" We earn our respect.

We hear all across the country all the time about the disrespect of students for teachers in classrooms. I make the claim, "Give me any class in any city. Give me the lowest-achieving students, those who have done poorly. Tell me nothing about those students, not even what they're studying, and I can go into that classroom and connect with those students."

You cannot fake it. Students may know nothing, they may be complete illiterates, but they know when we know, and they respect when we know. A good teacher must be more than a 2x4 teacher—bounded by the four walls of a classroom and the two covers of a book. I have a passion for being the very best teacher that I can be.

We say to our students, "I love you very much, but here you're either going to succeed or you're going to die. Now, take your choice." We do not allow children to fail. I constantly hear teachers saying the children fail. Well, do children ever fail in your school? We do not let them. Think for a moment—a child can stay home and get a U. A child can stay home and get an Incomplete. A child can stay home and fail.

What do six-, seven- or eight-year-old children know of what will happen to them in the future in terms of self-esteem and livelihood if they do not get an education? And I think those of us who have any modicum of success here today had some adult, some teacher, some parent, someone who did not allow us the privilege of failing. They always thought that just one more time would do it.

We hear constantly about the grammar of inner-city children, and "That's the way they are," and "That's the way they talk." Every child in our school is articulate. Every child speaks standard English, because when we go to the marketplace, that is the English that must be spoken. Any conversations (in my opinion) in black, white, green, or polka dot English is bound to be confusing. Our teachers are correcting consistently—all day, every moment, infinitely—throughout the entire year. We have been correcting the children's grammar until they realize that there is the standard grammar that must be spoken universally if we are going to function.

Many people say that what we do with our children is far too difficult. The critics complain much more. Usually, people are more comfortable with pre-packaged teachers' guides. They don't want to teach things like Plato's *Republic*, Dostoevski, Nietzsche, Aeschylus, and Euripides because those things involve teacher preparation. We have debates every two weeks. We have vocabulary contests with the entire school every other week. We have an author's contest every three weeks. Almost every child in our school can tell you who wrote a book even if he hasn't read it yet. We believe in exposure. We believe in letting inner-city children know that there's a wider world than the fettered and the decadent inner city. If this is all there is to their world, why bother to achieve?

We believe all of our eighth-graders matriculate at a twelfth-grade level. All of our textbooks are written on a twelfth-grade level or college freshman level, because we believe that when you aim low, there's really no place to go. I still believe that the grasp should not exceed the reach. You can take one group of students and teach them: "See Sue. See Pepper. See the ball. See the big ball. See the big red ball." Of course, they see it—there's a huge picture on the page.

Children who're new, children who have come into our school, will constantly look for picture clues. And the older child will say, "In this school you must read. There are no pictures in the text books." I tried to find textbooks that were old classics, with more and more print, rather than more and more pictures and less print. You can take one group of students and teach them: "See Sue. See the ball. See the big ball. See the big red ball." You take another group and you teach them Emerson's *Self-Reliance*, Thoreau, Dostoevski or Euripides; you're going to have a brighter group of children—not by genetics, not because of who their families are, not because they're on welfare, but because of what they have been exposed to.

I've been asked many times, "Well, what happens with children who come from very negative homes?" We will get a very negative parent in the beginning, and we notice that after two or three months, that parent's attitude begins to change. Our parents are constantly telling us that their children play teacher all the time at home. Whereas they used to come to school in the mornings constantly being told, "Sit down! Shut up! Don't do that!" they are now counting how many cars there are on the way to school. Depending on the age, they begin to read the street signs, or they're sounding out words. In fact, they have learned how to think and they want to learn how to think better.

I often notice parents who have very poor spelling in their notes they send to school at the beginning of the year. And then I notice that same parent, two, three, four, five, or six months later—the spelling improves. Their entire attitude about life becomes better.

We hear a lot about parents who do not care. But think for a moment: none of us wants to say that our children are incarcerated. None of us want to say that our children are in penal institutions. We'd all like to reply, "My son is a doctor. My son is a teacher. My son is a professional." Better than saying "My child's on drugs. My child has failed." People want to do better if only they can see a better way. We make certain that we give our parents the kind of school that they cannot find anywhere else in the world.

Many parents get aggravated by our policy that, "If you do not work, you do not eat." Our children learn that very well. It's more difficult for our parents. You only have to take a lunch from a child one day, and you feel sorry, and you want to give in. You see those big crocodile tears come and you really want to give him his lunch. But then you hear that kid tell another kid the next day, "You'd better get busy finishing that work because it's gonna soon be lunch time and here, if you don't work, you don't eat."

If we look at today's generation, it's "What's in it for me?" and it's "Give me." If we interview average young people today, they want to be millionaires by the time they're 30. And "How much can I do, and how much can I derive from this, and how little can I give back?" I think we all need money to survive, but we have to get with that spirit again where we want to give something back, where it's a legacy. It's our rent that we pay for our space on earth. We tell our children it's a shame to live an entire life and have no one ever know that you were here. And I don't mean creating crimes. That's average. Anybody can do that. It doesn't take any brains to take a gun and blow someone's head off. It doesn't take any brains to rape, to rob, to maim.

But it takes brains to be good doctors, to develop a cure for cancer, to make worthy, positive contributions to the world. And I think if we can continually and daily and consistently do this over and over—indoctrinate our children to this idea, we will see these things happening. In Chicago they have what they call the Gifted Program at Northwestern University on Saturdays. Our 9-, 10-, and 11-year olds are the youngest children in that program. But what would happen if I had not given them the tools to get into that program? What if I had not said, "Well, if you can do it in high school, it can also be done at a younger age."

We have 9-, 10- and 11-year-olds who matriculate at the University of Illinois' Saturday College. You know, the first thing they will tell you is, "My, this is going to look pretty good on my resume." These children are children who have thought about the future. When President Reagan came to visit our school, as many people do. . .(We have thousands of visitors each year, all coming to see a miracle. And it's anything but a miracle. We struggle. We have fewer facilities than most schools have. Most of the teachers and principals who visit us adjust the pictures on the walls of their architects' dreams and would build us another school. The only pictures you see on our walls are the children's papers. It's a school that belongs to the children, and there are no commercial products at all in our school; the school is theirs.). . .but when President Reagan came to visit us, a 5-year-old walked up to him and said, "Do you know who I am, Mr. President?" And he said, "No." (And you're shaking because you never know what our children are going to say next. And you pray for the President's sake that they'll say the right thing.) He told the president his name and he said, "I'm the brightest child in the whole world. Don't you want to be like me when you grow up?"

President Reagan looked in awe because our children come from the traditional single-family home. People say that we hand-pick our children and that's just not true. I can't think of any inner-city people who are wealthy, who have money to spend foolishly. We have welfare parents who really struggle to send their children to our school. We have parents who really work hard. It's a struggle for all of us. We struggle because we want a different life for one generation. We feel it begins with this generation. But our children look at famous people coming all the time, and they are respectful to them, but they never feel that somehow those people are greater than they, the children, are. Our children feel good about themselves. As a result, people are appalled we have no discipline problems.

When a new child starts to argue about a pencil, an older child who has been there longer will say, "Here, take this pencil. I'm trying to figure out how to own the whole pencil company." And as a result, we do not have the discipline problems that most schools have. Or a child will say to one another one, "You've taken away my right to learn." Well, that kind of disarms the devil who's trying to keep confusion in a classroom. Or if a child insists on acting up, we will say, "Why aren't you going to do that?" Their retort to us is, "Because I'm too bright to waste my time." We do not have our children write those ridiculous mundane lines: "I will not chew gum" or "I will not fight in school." If you notice, they're usually misspelled, half-written, with poor handwriting. What they have to do instead is find the etymology of *gum*—where the first gum came from. Those papers are graded. Or they have to stand up and give an impromptu three-minute speech on "Why I Am Too Bright To Waste My Time In School." We take every negative and make it a learning process.

In fact, one child insisted on kicking another under the desk. And when he went home, his mother called me at home that night. She said, "Johnny said would you please spank him because he has every book in the world out here on kicking." He had to do the etymology of *kick.* I think that when we use it in a positive framework, they are learning. She said, "You know, he's had me at the library. We don't have encyclopedias at home, but he says, 'Oh, no. I have to have this when I go to school in the morning.'"

We tell them that's their ticket in the door. I find that if we give them a positive reason and take that negative and make it a learning process, that they learn something during the interim. Because, usually when a child writes, "I will not chew gum," he will chew gum again. But I think if we can take that negative and turn it into a positive, it becomes a much better enterprise. When we talk about educating all of our children, we speak about what children can learn because of the kind of homes they come from. I had two or three of our former students get together with all the students over the Christmas holidays. I sat and I looked in that classroom as they all assembled there. (You know, you can hear the critics say that my expectations are too high, that I lie about what happens, that I lie about the test scores: but if you can just hang on long enough, you can somehow change what the critics say.) I thought about how every one of our students—every one since I started our school 13 years ago—has continued on. My students are now in college, in Eastern prep schools on $13,000 to $16,000 a year scholarships, or in Lake Forest Academy in Lake Forest, Ill. And we have letters on file where these people write and ask,

"Can you send us some more minds like the ones you've sent us?" Think of that for a moment. all the students who entered our school are either attending very good, fine, private, high schools, or are in college. And I think that's a record that no one can match now.

But think if I had given up, if I had listened to the critics. And it's rough. Sometimes it's very, very difficult because people yield very painfully to change. There's an attitude across this country that if your skin is black, it has something to do with achieving. It has something to do with what you can achieve. It has something to do with the contributions that you can make. And I sit and I think what contributions all of these children are going to make to society. They talk about being builders, about being bankers, about building their neighborhoods. You will see six-, seven-, and eight-year-olds reading *Barrons* (they play the stock market with play money) and the *Wall Street Journal.*

And it's because these are the things that I exposed them to, because I believed that they could. I believe that if we do not change one generation now, it shall become self-perpetuating where one generation is raised on welfare, the next comes up on welfare. All the children in our school will tell you that they never have to worry about welfare because they have learned how to say "Well." We do not have to teach our children about not getting pregnant. They have learned what they want from their lives. We have no time for sex-education classes, or drug-abuse classes. Our kids will tell you that they have too much to say yes to. We're supposed to tell children just say no to drugs, but what have we given them to say yes to? Today's children cannot read, write, think, or compute. We've raised them up without morals.

Everything in our school teaches perseverance, determination—not Horatio Alger stories that most of you young people here today have never heard of. The Horatio Alger story is about poor boys, or poor people making it good. We read stories of people making it against the odds, stick-to-it-iveness, determination, perseverance, honesty, keeping our word, things like *The Pied Piper of Hamelin.* Today's children know nothing about keeping their word. They actually think I xerox for all the teachers copies of the Ten Commandments. The average young person today thinks that Moses brought the Ten Suggestions from Mount Sinai. They actually think that we suggest that you do this or not do this—but these are *commandments*.

And then we complain. . .

I think young people have really gotten a rotten break. We talk about how terrible they are, but think of the diet of happy-ever-after stories in their schools. Well, you know we tell our children, "Kids, the castle leaks, the castle roof leaks, it has to be painted, the lawn has to be mowed—it has to be maintained." If we think about it, the government helped get us in this mess. Never could so many people have failed in their lives if they had not had help from the government. I know many of us do not want to hear this, but I think of Abraham Lincoln, who was 14 when he started school and when he learned to read. And he used to sit before the log fire, according to history (all we know is what we read) and say, "Abraham Lincoln has hand and pen, and he'll be good, but only God knows when." If he were in today's school, can you realize he would be put into a learning-disability room? You know, I chastise educators as I go across the country, and I lecture to this group of At Risk teachers of the At Risk students. We've had so many At Risk students that now we've been called A Nation At Risk. If a student is At Risk, what are we doing to remove that risk?

I hear teachers and educators complaining about how far a child is behind; what a child doesn't know. That's one thing every teacher at my school is fortunate that she has never heard. That's what we're there for. It's not a problem. You can see it as a problem, or you can see it as a challenge. Give me the child nobody else wants, who nobody else has been able to teach to read or to do whatever—that's a child who can be saved. Now, many of you will say, "Well, you know naturally you can do that in your own school, but you don't metamorphose into a different person in a different ambience."

I was the same kind of teacher in the public schools. The children were poor—they were inner-city children—but I insisted that they rise to my expectations. I had one little girl whose mother was an alcoholic. She had missed (I looked in her records) 101 days (There were only 181 days in the school year) of the previous year. When I got her in my class, she came to school every day. One day I noticed her dress was on the wrong side out. I whispered in her ear and I said, "Carol, sweetheart, your dress is on the wrong side out." She said, "I know, Mrs. Collins, but I didn't want to miss school, and it was dirty on the other side." You see what we can do.

It's the dirty kid whom education sits in the back of the room and keeps sending to the office; it's the dirty kid who destroys society. Those are the kids you must touch. Those are the ones you make friends with. We always hear about the discipline problems in today's schools. It's because you do not touch a child when he's in trouble if you've never established some rapport with him before. You know, Ralph Waldo Emerson said, "Man is constantly astounded by common sense." And that's so true. People come to our school— pay air fares—from all over the world to come to be trained or to come to visit, and all they see is common sense, old-fashioned American dedication, bright, caring teachers, and action. That's all there is to see—in a building that's too small for its participants.

But I'm amazed by how we have somehow lost all semblance of common sense in this country. We've let the experts tell us what's best for our children. What we must remember—it's the experts who got us into the mess that we're in now. It's the experts who have written the textbooks, who have written the teacher's manuals, who certify the teachers. And I certainly say to each of you who are in the teaching profession or who plan to go into the teaching profession: Remember that you innately have all the right stuff that it takes to make a good teacher, if you eradicate yourself of the idea that these children cannot learn. Think of great teachers like Annie Sullivan, who taught Helen Keller. Give me the child who's a challenge.

Almost all teachers can teach the bright child, but can you motivate the devil? The devil needs to be in school, not at home. You know, anybody can send a child to the office; that's a very poor teacher. The superior teacher always has the idea (the opinion) that just one more time will do it; and if that doesn't work, to walk up to a child, hug him and say, "Look, I love you very much, but you're going to get your act together. You're going to learn or you're going to die. Now, you take your choice." Children respect the fact that you care. They rebel against order, but they respect nothing else. They tell us that they want the easy way, that they want to get by. I used to say to children in the public schools, "You know, when you're in this classroom, why do you behave? Why do you stop when you see me?" And they would tell me, "Because we know that you won't take it." I would say, "I don't hit you. How do you know?" They said, "All you need to do is look at us." But I think somehow they know who they can get by, and if you lose them (those of you who are going into teaching), if you lose a child on Day One, you can forget it. You will not get that class back again. They respect the fact that you maintain your own classroom.

Many of the things that the experts have taught many of you—well, many of those experts have never taught a day in their lives. Think about it when you line children up to go to the wash room. Children are bright enough to know when they have to use the wash room. I have three children. I never remember lining them up to go to the wash room. They were intelligent enough to know when they had to go. No child in our school (I didn't do it in the public schools) asks us to go to the wash room. It becomes just setting militaristic roles to line children up all day. It's about all we get done. You'll find when all 30 (or 32, 25, etc., if you have them) of the children's bladders just don't go off at the same time. And we say that something is too difficult for them today, but watch the average children when they come into our school, I will ask them, "Do you know Michael Jackson's 'Beat'?" And they'll say, "I do! I do! Mrs. Collins," and they think that they're pleasing me. And I'll say,

"Sing it for me." They will mimic and say from memory every line. I'll say, "Very good. If you can do that, you can learn Chaucer's *Canterbury Tales* in Middle English, too." It's almost gone the way of the last dinosaur, but the average young child today wants some. That becomes your teacher's guide. Almost all of them know every video and they know every song on the radio. The three- and four-year-olds can mimic every radio and television commercial. What makes us think they cannot memorize poetry too? You know, I think our children are almost the only children in this country who still memorize: *Trees* and *House By the Side of the Road*: "Let me live in a house by the side of the road and be a friend to man"; or *Invictus*: "Out of the night that covers me/black as a pit from hole to hole/I thank whatever God may be/for my unconquerable soul."

Then there's Henry Wadsworth Longfellow's poem (They've learned about keeping your word) where a little boy is dying. His mother left him to care for (when she died) his 9-year-old brother. He borrowed money from a gentleman to buy a loaf of bread because his brother is hungry, and a train hits him on the way back to carry the money back to the gentleman. He gives it to his brother just before he dies and says, "Be sure and pay that man back because I promised." These are lessons our children today know nothing about. It's not their fault. They have not grown up on, "Do unto others as you would have them do unto you."

We have the shopping centers, we have so many things to do on Sundays, they just do not get to church anymore. Yet we've removed the values from our schools, and we wonder why they behave the way they do. We're expecting them to behave the way we think they should behave, because we grew up on certain values. But these children have not been exposed to these values. You can only do as you know how to do. Sure, we can talk about the parents who do not care, but if we do not change the children, then we all are doomed. Think that today's children (miseducated) will one day lead us. You know, I find myself looking in the cockpit of airplanes to see if the pilot looks literate. It sounds funny, but it's very important to me.

I try to select my doctors today who are old enough to have killed enough patients to know what they're doing. It gets very scary because we are in a just-good-enough attitude generation. We tell our children, "If you are a doctor and they cut two centimeters to the right, it doesn't mean 'I guess' or 'I think.'" It means exactly two centimeters to the right. I think that we have to get back to that precision, that doing it right again. We see it in every area of society. Try to get someone to work for you at your house—paid to do repairs. Nobody takes the pleasure of doing it *right* anymore. We don't have that pride anymore: "That's my work."

Think what we tell students: "Every eighth-grader knows that you can fool around; you can play around. But, kid, unless we can put that Westside Preparatory School stamp on you, you do not leave this school. You do not leave this school until your reading score is at least 10.7 years. Your math score must be the same, or you will stay here until you are as old as Methuselah." If I did become Secretary of Education, one of the things I would do is pay the teachers more, or have a national ceremony for good teachers. And children would not be allowed to leave school until they had the skills. And if you don't come to school so many days per year, kid, the police will be at your house to get you. I think if we do not do that, we are constantly going to have an increase in the homeless, the have-nots. I do what I do very selfishly, because I would feel very comfortable having our children as my doctors, my attorneys.

We have to be very careful about where we send them to school, because they intimidate many teachers after they leave us. But they're constantly proofreading with us when we're writing at the blackboard: "You forgot a semi-colon. You forgot your quotation marks." But it shows they are paying attention, that they are in school for the right reason: to learn.

Of course, we are never intimidated by that. We will say

to students, "You are so bright," and that's where the kid got that for President Reagan—"Don't you want to be like me when you grow up?" We always say, when they correct us, "You are so bright. I want to be just like *you* when I grow up." We don't have discipline problems because the students constantly proofread with us. Of all the adults, educators, and superintendents that have read my book, it was a fourth-grader who came to me and pointed out that I had attributed a quotation to Aesop, and he told me that Aesop did not say it—DeLafontaine said it.

It shows that they are thinking. These are going to be the creators; these are the children I will be comfortable having as my doctors. I wanted to create citizens in my own school whom I would want as my neighbors, whom I would want as my friends, whom I would want as my doctors, whom I would want as my surgeons, whom I would want as my lawyers because they are precise. They take pride in what they do.

When a new student turns in a paper, our teachers will ask, "Would you give this paper to God?" If the child says "No," we don't want it either. We let them know whatever they do must be the very, very best that they can do. "If you were any attorney, would you be proud of this as a brief? Would you go to a doctor where the paper's all tattered and there's blood all over the records? Is that the kind of doctor you want?" Would you go to that doctor?

When we talk about how terrible the children are today, I think we all have to assume responsibility again. Would we want to go to a doctor who had a history of having killed 2,000 patients last year? Yet we keep having these school districts that continue to fail children.

Yet we can continue to work in that atmosphere. I think each of us here (those of you who are going into teaching) take the attitude that you can only do one day at a time. You can't teach a whole year in one day. Prepare to be the very best teacher you can be that one day, in that classroom. Then come home Day One and prepare to be the very best teacher you think you can be on Day Two. You can only teach one day at a time. But make certain that you are not going to add to the negative attitude that it's the children's fault.

You know, we certainly get by with that education. I don't know of any other profession that, when it fails, blames those whom it set out to help. Do lawyers keep saying, "Well, it's the client's fault"? Do doctors keep saying "It's the patient's fault," or do surgeons keep saying, "It's the patient's fault," or airline pilots keep saying, "It's the passengers' fault?"

I used to stay out of the teacher's lounge—and you might try doing that—because that's where I heard all of the negative doomsday cries about what the kids couldn't do. "Oh, these terrible kids today! Oh, these awful kids!" And no one wanted to talk to me because I wanted to talk about what Johnny was now doing or what this child was. Of course, when I came in, the entire room became hush-hush. I was the bad guy because I expected the very best from those children, and I got it. If I took them to the cafeteria and they threw the food, I marched their little bodies back to the classroom rather than have them sit at other tables, because I figured you don't throw food if you're hungry. I would get into trouble with the principal because all he wanted them to do was eat. It didn't matter to him how they ate. But it mattered to me because ignoring it is saying negative behavior is right. Then we wonder why they end up destroying society.

If it took me 20 minutes to get them down the steps, I'd march them up and down until they realized they mustn't run. They'd say, "Oh! The principal is going to get you. You're supposed to be out of here at 3." Sure enough, the principal did get me. But I made certain that they realized that was a certain rule. There are rules in the world. If you do not obey them, there's a place called jail. Unfortunately, I think children learn that later in life. Rather than sitting with the teachers every day. I always rotated and changed, eating with a different group of students every day, so I got to know all my students. All the other principals and teachers would wonder why my students didn't call me names, but I became their friends before they were in trouble. You don't just run up and collar a child when you don't know his name.

When I taught school, I would sit outside when the weather was nice and talk with the students—get to know them. You're already friends with the teachers; they're not going to bother you. Yet my principal would be critical because I didn't fraternize with the teachers. Well, you know, you're going to get rough on one end or the other. But I did fraternize with the children. That's what my job is. That's what I was paid for. I would go on the playground. We'd see all the fights on the playground. I would go on the playground at recess time with my children. The other teachers would go and get their coffee and their rolls. I would go outside and join hands with the children.

I would hold the child who never engaged in the games. You know, there's always a child—kids can be very cruel— that does not get included in their games. I would always grab the dirty child's hand. The child whom the kids didn't want to play with, and you know what happened? Without a word being said, that kid became popular with the other children, because they'd say, "Well, if Mrs. Collins likes him, I guess I have to like him in order for her to like me." So, I'd say, "You don't want to hold his hand. That's O.K. You just don't know what you're missing. I'll hold his hand." Then we'd get in line. We'd get in the games. My children in the public schools (of course, in my own school, we have no recess and gym) never had a yard fight. Why? Because I was there.

How can one aide oversee thousands of children on the playground at play time? And children are children; they are going to get into spats. If you look in your guide [tips to young teachers], you'll see advice to look in your garbage pails when the kids are gone. Do you see the notes? Do you see the ones who are going to beat Jamie up after school? So you keep Jamie and you send Johnny home, and they can't fight.

I have also learned to go in the girls' washroom (this sounds like espionage) and sit on the stool with my feet up, so I can hear the conversations in the girls' washroom. You find out how they think what's going on, and then you are better able to work with it. They would ask me, "How do you know that?" I would say, "O.K. let's get all of (if they were high school kids) these divorces out of the way today, so that we can get rid of the attitudes." They'd say, "How do you know that? How do you know who likes who?" And I'd say, "Oh! I know everything." But they never realized that I was in that girls' wash room.

But I guess what I'm saying—it's the attitude. It's the positive attitude, and I do what I do with a passion. If I had the money, I would never have to do lectures like these. I would just like to stay and work with those children because they have something. My adrenaline gets going. I feel 20 years younger. I forget all my problems. I forget everything. I think you don't know what can really happen when you know. Think of the power—and we talk about how terrible teaching is—but think of the power that you possess to manage a whole group of children. You can bend them like a piece of putty. You can make them what you want. When I read a story, the kids are getting out of their seats. I make it come alive. You know, they'll tell me that when we have teacher trainees—they don't tell me in front of you, but they say "I don't like the way they read it. They don't make it come alive the way you-all do."

If you're teaching history, you have to make it come alive. If you're teaching math, and if you want to alleviate the discipline problems—remove yourself from the pre-packaged lesson plans. For example, we'll take an entire group of children and we'll go "Seven times three! Plus two! Divided by four! Minus six! Plus eight!" Every child is listening because the next child knows that he or she is It. But it's the verbal things that somehow we have forgotten today. We do the listening activities. "If Dostoevski wrote *The Brothers Karamazov*, write your last name three times on line five of this paper. If Dostoevski did not write *The Brothers Karamazov*, write the sum of seven plus seven minus four, divide it by six, times eight on line 13 of your paper. If neither of these are true, write the number that comes after 99 on the fifth line of your paper."

And you see, children must listen to do those things. These are not things that I got from textbooks. These were things that I have devoted my life to. I want to know. I teach every day. Every teacher in my school teaches every day. We have to because we are under high visibility. We have visitors all the time. Every other school in America can do it wrong, but we must do it right because we get criticized, and we're watched all the time. But teach every day. Do whatever profession you're in, do it every day, every moment, as if the whole world were watching. I teach as if Jesus Christ Himself were in that classroom. And when you do that, you're bound to see great things happening. But if you go in with the attitude that it's not going to make a difference. . . .

For every class I've ever taught, you'll find adults who do not understand me. But you can't find one child in this country who says he doesn't like Mrs. Collins. I can lead them in my neighborhood to hell and back. I can lead the children in our school. If I tell them I want a piece of the sky, they'll just say, "How quickly do you want it?" And that's a rapport that you establish by letting them know that you truly care about them. Yet, because you care about them, you want them to be all that they can possibly be. And they know when it's important to you. I say to any kid in our school who insists on failing, "You know, one day you're going to want grow up and be President of the United States, and they're going to say, 'No, because you killed Mrs. Collins because you wouldn't learn.' You're going to apply for a job, and they're going to say, 'No.' Everything that you attempt to do, Kid, they're going to say, 'No, because you killed Mrs. Collins.'" These kids soon learn that you truly care. Children who come to our school tell their parents, "I like that school because there they do hard work."

Morley Safer tried to connive a child into saying he didn't like our school. He said: "Why do you like this school? It's so hard here. There's no recess. There's no gym. They work you all day. You have only 40 minutes for lunch. Why do you like it? It's just too hard." And the student said, "That's why I like it, because it makes your brains bigger."

And I think that's what they really want—they have really not asked for this to be watered down. They like to know that they know something, that they can help other people. As soon as children in our school learn to read and compute on a certain level, they must sign a list of where they have helped four other people in their neighborhoods, in their housing projects, in their area.

We took 60 children from the infamous Cabrini-Green Housing Project on a scholarship, and the bus driver wouldn't stop for them because he had heard how terrible they talked. And they were awful! We rode the buses with them for the first three weeks. After they had been there about three months, the bus driver came into the school one day and said, "I've heard a lot about this school and about you, but I want you to know that when those kids first got on the bus, they would say every kind of name, they'd call people everything you could think of, and the language they used was unspeakable." He said, "But now, they get on there in the afternoons and they're reciting poetry. They are saying, 'I'll bet you didn't know this.' They're reading books. They're just completely different children."

Each of us can make a difference. Each of us has what it takes to make a difference—and that's a passion for being excellent in what we do. That's a passion for doing what we do so well that nobody else can do it. And it's certainly not being average. All of us are what we are, and are where we are, because of the excellence of somebody before us. I ask you to think about those people who helped you. Be all that you can be. Think how you can pass it on.

And most of all, and most selfishly, think that if we do not begin to relight the candles of excellence in America, the people who are miseducated today will lead us tomorrow. And right now, that seems to be a pretty sorry state. So, I ask each of you: "Won't you do all that you innately have the possibilities and the capabilities to do and relight the candles of excellence in America."

With all our problems, it's still the greatest country on earth. It's the only country we have, so won't you please do that?

Thank you and God Bless You!

3.
Strong Minds for the Future

Thousands of visitors journey to Chicago to visit our facility, and they all declare it a miracle. We call it common-sense. What others call breaking "New Ground," we here at Westside Preparatory School call cultivating "Old Ground"—instilling old values and morals so that we are not consumed in the future by adults who grew up on perennial overdoses of mediocrity and failure. Most importantly, we believe that even if we manage to teach our children to read, write, and think critically and analytically, we also must teach them morality so that we are not led in the future by a norm-less society, or a "Do-Your-Own-Thing" generation.

What other schools declare as learning disabilities, we at Westside Preparatory School believe are teacher inabilities. We take the failure of any student very seriously, for we realize that the students who are educated, or miseducated, in today's classrooms will one day lead us. What then? We do not adhere to the mucilaginous excuses for student failure. We have not become anesthetized to the doomsday cries that our children will never amount to very much anyway; so why bother? We realize that we must *bother to realize* that all children are champions worth wrestling. If we do not believe in our own children, why must we expect others to see them as diamonds when we ourselves could only see them as lumps of worthless coal. We believe that every student is coal in the raw with the potentials of becoming diamonds illuminating light.

In our issue-a-week-society, when others become mesmerized with "We Are The World," "Olliemania," and "I Got A Peek At The Pope," and "What Will Vanna Wear

Tonight," we here at Westside Preparatory keep our eyes on our major goal. . .our children. We realize that our own future is inextricably woven in the threads of what our children are. We have refused to have our students become viscid images that we allow to flit through our fast-edit consciousness without passion or compassion.

In other words, our students are extensions of each of us. We always want to be proud to say: "These are our students; when cometh more?"

4

All The World is a Stage. . .We Each Play Our Roles in Life

As William Shakespeare said, "All the world is a stage and we each play our parts. . .we have our exits and entrances." Life is pretty much like a comedy or a Greek tragedy, or just plain drama. Some of us are major role players, and some of us are understudies. Some of us play minor roles in life. Some of us receive standing ovations, and some of us are never known at all. What makes the difference? What makes our roles so different in life?

The people who are the major role players in life receive the standing ovations because they see the hurdles of life as stepping stones. The people who play the minor roles in life are those who see the hurdles of life as stumbling blocks. The players of life who receive the thunderous and unending standing ovations are those who remove the "t" from "can't," and design a whole new philosophy that says, "I can and I will do what others declare impossible."

The understudies of life are those who are pretty much like the characters that inhabit Plato's *Republic*, cave dwellers who have been immersed in darkness for so long that they have begun to embrace it as a comfortable reality. One inhabitant is dissatisfied with his world and takes it upon himself to discover alternatives to his murky, dark world. Seeing a light in the distance, he comes out of the darkened cave and declares that there is light outside, but the comfortable cave dwellers who have taken darkness as a way of life declare the light-finder a charlatan and foolish idealist. His fellow troglodytes find that the light dazzles them just a bit too much, and they choose to remain locked in a pool of darkness and ignorance, never knowing the joy of light and freedom.

Some people enter the stage of life and play their roles with aplomb in pleasure and in pain. Exiting before giving a command performance is unheard of for them. When the times get a bit rough in a world that girdles us all about and puts all sorts of hard questions to us, the minor role players of life decide that exiting the difficult stage of life is easier than bearing the whips and scorns of life. The minor role players in life decide that success comes quickly and slickly packaged. The major role players in life know that life by the inch is a cinch; life by the yard is hard. They also realize that *difficult* does not mean *impossible*. They are motivated in knowing that the roads to success must be paved with their own vision, and not vision that is borrowed. They further realize that the road to success may be new, and that they will suffer, they will fight, they will pay, but ultimately they win. The minor role players in life are not willing to fight. . .to pay. . .to suffer, and so, they never win.

The minor role players in society wait for their motivation to be delivered by others. The major role players bring their own will to win; they are self-motivated, self-generated, and self-propelled.

The minor role players in society talk constantly of luck. The major role players believe that their pluck in life is their luck. The minor role players believe that God will provide. The major role players know that God is not a cosmic bellboy who comes at their beck and call, and that the bounties of life will not be served to them on proverbial platters. They know that the first steps to success must be their own undertaking. They are never marooned by the difficult. They are inspired by the "can'ts" of others, making them their "cans."

The major role players in life take the lemons of life and make lemonade. The minor role players see only the lemons with a "Why-me?" attitude rather than a "Why Not Me?" attitude.

The minor role players are always uncomfortable with

riding the back of the tiger for fear of ending up inside the tiger's mouth. The minor role players wait for others to bring success to them already wrapped in a neatly tied package. In other words, the minor role players of life believe more in distribution rather than in creation. They have never learned that creation must always come before distribution, or there will be nothing to distribute.

The minor role players of life are always complaining and crying doomsday cries. The major role players of life lament to no one, for they realize that their weeping in life falls on deaf ears and that, in the end, they are the only ones who can solve their problems.

The minor role players of life feel that one dose of success lands them in the Land of the Done; the major role players of life know that success is not a destination, but an unending journey that will always have them in the stress of doing, achieving, succeeding and achieving. They, in other words, never develop "That's Good Enough" attitude.

When the awards of life are given out for splendid performances, the minor role players sit on the sidelines of life lamenting about how lucky the major role players are, and how unfair life is. They are envious because, on the day of victory, few of us are tired. They feel that they have been cheated by life, never admitting that life will pay any price we ask. If we go through life with a bargain price on our efforts, that then, is all we will receive. The minor role players in life have come to realize that no bird flies too high who soars with his or her own wings.

The Home Tutor

Responsibility is often thought of as a fourth "R." We can teach reading, writing and arithmetic here, but much of the responsibility for your child's education must come from home. Being a responsible student means making the right choices. It means paying attention to the teacher's directions, it means doing nightly homework, and doing just a little more work than the teacher assigned.

Remember, school is a microcosm of the real world. The

reason most schools do not work is that school is just the opposite of what is expected of citizens in the real world. This, therefore, means that a child must practice being above average in school so that they can take what they've learned into the real world.

This means giving each task in school a real effort, not just doing enough to squeeze by.

Most experts agree that responsibility is learned from parents. Here are some suggestions for using the "example" and "practice" method that will allow you, the parent, to teach your child responsibility.

Let your child help you with household chores. As you work together, be clear about the purpose of each task. Praise your child for the good efforts and positively point out the negatives by saying, "I think you can do this better, don't you?" Explain that if you do not polish the furniture that the wood will crack and dry out. This allows the child to learn that most things we do have a cause and effect. Thus the child comes to learn that some actions have consequences attached to them.

Point out to your child that you, the parent, work when there are other things you would rather do. Show a child how to do a task correctly, and be patient as your child learns.

Teach your child organization. Make certain that each night, at the completion of the day's homework, all materials are put away and ready for the next day of school. This means getting shoes and other personal items together and all in one place so that the next morning will not be filled with the frustration of: "You are going to be late."

Teach your child to be time-oriented. Remember, in the real world, the workplace will not tolerate tardiness and excuses. Therefore, teach your child to accept responsibility for his or her actions, and not to make excuses for shortcomings.

Make certain that you discuss the day's activities with your child on a daily basis. This can be done while eating, driving to school, getting the child dressed or any activity within the home.

5.
Freedom and What
it Means to Me

Wars have been fought because of it. Societies have revolted in search of it. Tocqueville tried to define it in his book, *Democracy in America*. Patrick Henry declared that if he could not have it he preferred death. People are incarcerated unjustly because of the lack of it, and hopes and self-esteem are snuffed out when it is missing. What is it? It is a thing called freedom. Many of us take it for granted until we become a victim of not having enough of it. Children defy parents because they feel that they have not received enough of it.

Though we complain loud and long about our lack of freedom in America, we are still fortunate when we compare our country to other countries. With all of our problems, America is still the greatest country on earth. The magnificent dream started in 1776 is still alive today. If the American nightmare seems to be outdistancing the American dream it is because we, as Americans, stopped dreaming, and we became comfortable with our preeminence as a world leader, and many of us thought that good meant forever. In other words, we rested on our past laurels as a free country. Those of us who truly care about our place in the sunlight of the American dream are out here daily doing all that we can to save the greatest country on earth—America.

This is still the country of dreams, and despite all of the doomsday cries from all sides all of us are still imbedded in the American dream, and when dreams die, Langston Hughes told us, "Life is a barren field filled with snow, life is a broken-winged bird that cannot fly." So let us together dare to hold fast to the American dream. Let us begin to know that we were promised the pursuit of freedom and happiness, and that is what we must do. We must continually pursue freedom for ourselves; it will not be served us on a proverbial platter.

Many Americans have assumed the proposition that God is some cosmic bellboy that will come at our beck and call, and that God was put into the sky to answer our daily incantations, but God's work on earth must truly be our own.

Freedom is never an easy enterprise, nor is maintaining freedom a simple task. Mediocrity, complacency, and a general lowering of standards are and have always been the antagonists of freedom in the saga of human life.

Freedom, personally to me, is the right to choose. The right to choose the good life over becoming a failing leaner. I believe that all citizens deserve the inalienable right to be able to raise their families in dignity and self-esteem, and I believe that the classrooms of every American school must become the flames that will enlighten the world, fire the imagination, give might to dreams and wings to the aspirations of girls and boys so that they may dare to become literate citizens of their locales and, with equal comfortableness, citizens of the universe. I believe that far too few educators realize that a good, solid education is the parent of progress, the creator of creativity, the designer of opportunity and the molder of human destiny.

This period and time in history demands much of us. These are the times that will maroon the hesitant, but it is also a period that will inspire those of us who still believe in the American dream, and who still believe in freedom in all of its glorious forms. The more we believe this, the more we will realize that tyranny and injustice, like Hell, are not easily conquered.

We all have a capacity to know the glory of human deeds. Today demands deeds: human deeds. All of us must become courageous in spirit through pleasure or in pain to realize that the command of reason toward freedom is the holy fire that keeps our purposes warm and our intelligence aglow.

Emma Lazarus penned: "Give me your huddled masses yearning to breathe freedom and I will give them peace.". .let us then begin to reach out of our vacuumed, air-tight compartments and oil our long-locked, rusty hearts to reinstate freedom to those huddled masses still yearning to breathe the freedom promised them. . .To delay in our mission is to, in the end, shackle all freedom-loving Americans. Each of us must begin to carry the banner of freedom to the last hour. It matters nothing in the history of a race as to who in their time carried the banner of free men. What matters is that the battle shall and must go on. We cannot, however, know the promises of the joys of Elysium without national effort. Our reluctance to act collectively for the freedom of all of us shall paralyze all of us into retreat rather than advance. The cry of distress is heard on all sides, but those of us to whom more has been given, more is expected. We therefore must not allow those cries of distress to ring hollow.

We will all commit a sin of omission if we do not utilize the fiber and core of our hearts to buttress our fragile segments of society where freedom is missing. None of us can afford to isolate ourselves in a kind of age of the shrug, with a "So what, it's not my problem" attitude. All of us are the heirs of all ages. None of us can afford to overlook the uglier side of our inheritance. We all together must help to eradicate the legacy of abuse, degradation, the inhumanity of men blinded by prejudice, ignorance, and personal spleen. To those of us who care, this is a special legacy and a challenge to accept the uglier side of life as well as the beautiful, and to answer this challenge is indeed a privilege and a responsibility. The only way we can achieve our own freedom and happiness is to strive for the happiness of others. Brotherhood and freedom must cease to be a sentimental, mushmouthed, super-hyperglycemic phrase. We must begin to realize that the brotherhood of man exists as emphatically as does the fatherhood of God.

It is the responsibility of all great Americans to begin to forge the keys that will stir ambition. To stimulate ideas and disarm anarchy. We must all become sources of inspiration. The aid of inspiration. The forces of positive determination that will one day promise to become the hope of the young, the joy of age and the hope of our adolescents. We must all become the parents of progress, the creators of culture and the molders of freedom so that our children, too, will one day continue to carry the unfurled banner of freedom. Together in the name of freedom, we must all do what we can to eradicate the stripes of failure, the pangs of hunger, and then we shall bear in triumph the wisdom of all ages, by making today different so that others may dare to dream of a tomorrow shining brightly under amber and spacious skies known as America.

6.
Hopes Enunciated and Principles Expressed

The books *Closing of the American Mind*, by Bloom; *Cultural Literacy in America*, by E.D. Hirsch, Jr.; and a recent publication, *The Classic Touch*, by John K. Clemens, which attempt to teach lessons in leadership from Homer to Hemingway to the Business Community, are all great books. We have been teaching these lessons to our children all the time at Westside Preparatory School.

The irony of the situation is that I have actually been punished by the bureaucratic system for attempting to declare that inner-city children, too, can become leaders rather than failing learners. To dare to make such a statement seems to be so ridiculous to many Americans that one must be labeled controversial or a liar at most if we dare to declare that "Where one leaves his shoes at night has nothing to do with what he can become." I have never believed that poverty had anything to do with the brain. I have never believed that the kind of home, neighborhood, or ambience one comes from has anything to do with what he can become. In other words, I personally feel that the homeless, the miseducated, the disenfranchised are suffering from stolen self-esteem and self-determination. I used the word "stolen" because many of our citizens did not intentionally and voluntarily give their lives to miseducation. It was more or less planned failure, taught failure, and lowered expectations that somehow became Stanined, ink-blotted, and measured until these citizens were "pushed-out" of school. They did not voluntarily drop out. They were "pushed-out" to make room for more federally-funded failures.

For some years, I personally have taught a class called "Prepping for Power." My third-, fourth-, and fifth- grade students learned the tragedy of the seven deadly sins inherent in *Macbeth*. We learned of the indecisiveness of Hamlet from Shakespeare's play, *Hamlet*. We learned that there is no greed like the greed of thinking that something is free. From *The Iliad*, we learned how the Greeks thought that a "freebie" would surely fool the Trojans, and it did. Beware of riding the back of the tiger or we might end up inside the tiger's mouth.

We learned the lessons of Machiavelli in the fourth grade. We realize that power seldom gives in to the lower masses. We learned from Voltaire's *Candide* that if we want the best of all worlds, we must be willing to pay the price. In other words, we learned from almost every classic the meaning of hard work, determination, sense of purpose and most of all we learned, "There are no free rides in the world."

These lessons, I suppose, are an anachronism for inner-city children. Allegedly, this is the population which will always find themselves facing a carpet of glass rather than a carpet of grass, right? Wrong. Our students are learning how to become lifters of the American dream rather than failing learners reaping the American nightmare.

No employer will ever have to fear hiring our children for fear that our children will make poor risks or poor employees. This assertion was mentioned in Bloom's book, *Closing of the American Mind*. In other words, our children will be an asset to any employer, to their locales, and they will, with equal comfortableness, embrace and understand the distant drums of the universe.

Visitors from all over the world visit our school and exclaim, "I have never seen anything like it." Do they really mean to flatter us? Or, are they saying, "We did not believe that inner-city, poor children could learn?" Or does this mean that our children have fallen at the bottom of every statistic tabulated because the expectations for their success was too low?

We have trained 3,700 teachers at Westside Preparatory

School in our methodology in just a year and a half, and every teacher, principal and administrator states, "The problem with our schools is that our expectations are too low." Just as people are what they eat, we are what we learn. If we teach students the banalities of "See Sue, See Pepper, See Pepper run," of course we turn their brains into macaroni. In other words, we choke them on overdoses of illiteracy. Teach children, on the other hand, the classics such as Emerson's *Self-Reliance*, Thoreau's *What I Lived For*, and the work ethics learned in "The Ants and the Grasshopper," "The Little Red Hen," and Epictetus' lessons on ethics and leadership, and we will have different students. Not because of better genes, but because they, too, have a chance to be exposed to thought-provoking materials rather than the "See me picture-clue junk" we use in far too many of our American Schools.

To let students articulate "My mother, she be pretty" and think that is their culture and not correct their grammar and yet write on their papers "incorrect grammar" is tyrannical at most and quixotic at least. Correct their grammar every day, and when it is time to write, they will not have to think by the mile and become forced to write by the inch. Simple, huh? Common sense? Right. Emerson said, "Man is astounded by common sense."

While most schools are still teaching their five-year-olds to see the ball, see the cat, etc., we are teaching our children phonetics so that they will have the reading skills necessary to become readers by Christmas. We feel that they can draw and color the picture of an alphabet infinitely and never know the sound or how to make the letter if we do not remove ourselves from our Utopian authoritative desks and teach them. In other words, "see the ball, see the cat" is not a difficult exercise since there is usually a large picture of the item to "see," which gives the children a picture clue, and they are really not reading at all.

Our three- and four-year-olds use a vocabulary book titled, *Vocabulary for the High School Student*. Ridiculous? Maybe, but somehow the children love learning new words.

We also notice that the vocabulary of their parents change, too. One teaches another, you know—the Socratic philosophy.

Meanwhile, our students are learning the lesson inherent in the tale of the frogs who learn that it is easy to jump down into a well, but it is not easy to jump out. There are no picture clues, and the children must be able to read. Each selection read has a moral ending and a moral lesson. These lessons will take them through life, not just a reading exercise to fill the school day. If school is not a miniature society in which children can learn to practice for the real world, why do we continue to pay a bastion of teachers and administrators? Our children could become the miserable failures that they are without schooling.

Abraham Lincoln did not learn to read until he was fourteen years of age. If he had lived in our progressive days, today, he never could have become President of the United States, for he would have had to bear the label of *learning disabled* or some other tag or label of our time until we ran out of letters in our educational lexicon. Of course, the federal government aids educators tremendously in their efforts to fail children, for without the government's help, we never could have done such a miserable job of educating our children. A few years ago, we declared that we had no problems in our schools, and then along came federal funds, and we said, "Maybe we do have a few problems, but nothing that a few federal dollars will not cure." Soon, very few children were considered normal.

Taxpayers spent $785,000.00 for the report "A Nation at Risk." I had already told them the same thing in my book *Marva Collins' Way*, and the price is only $12.95. This study told us that we have a nation of illiterates. We knew that already! So what are our solutions?

7.
Let Us Once Again
Let Freedom Ring in America

Socrates said, "The unexamined life is not worth living." I feel that we started to examine how we rear and educate our children. I am not a dewy-eyed nostalgic person, but I think of the times when children memorized nursery rhymes. When parents read bedtime stories to their children, when favorite poems were memorized and when families had the time to discuss these poems during dinner time—that was, of course, before videos, microwave ovens, and, of course, fast-food chains.

I recently overheard a four-year-old youngster singing, "I am looking for a new love baby," one of the popular tunes of the month, and I thought to myself: "There was a time when children sang London Bridges, or Little White Duck." What a difference progress makes, or should we call it recidivism? Have we learned how to fly and forgotten how to walk? Have we stripped our children of past literacy in the name of today's fast-track ambience?

Remember a few years ago how lessons were prefaced with "Casey at the Bat"; "Paul Revere's Ride"; *Aesop's Fables*; and "The Boy Who Cried Wolf"? The classics that taught us the hard knocks of life and perseverance? Today's basal readers in our schools teach our children the easy-to-read, easy-to-explore, easy-to-teach banalities of Dick and Jane running through their readers accomplishing the mundane daily activity of building dog houses and asking if we see the big red ball.

The term "Magnificent Dream" started in 1776 means nothing to our children today. They do not realize that our country was founded in 1776, and they have no idea how the country came to be founded. Doubt me? Ask your children and see if they can respond. Today's generation does not seem to realize what continent we live on—never mind the other six.

Remember when we could identify the great marches of our time? John Phillip Sousa and his march "Thunderer," and the other great marches such as "Stars and Stripes Forever"? Our children are completely illiterate of the past, and, therefore, one must wonder what the future holds for us with them as our caretakers.

Lucretius told us in his essay on the Nature of Things that nothing from nothing leaves nothing. We have given our children nothing—are we ready for the perennial reaping of nothing? What does it take for us to realize that all of our lives hang in a perilous vacuum? What does it take for us to realize that which Plato reminded us: "Education is cumulative and it affects the breed." What kind of breed are we nurturing in the name of progress?

As a very frightened American, I beg each of you to please undo the heavy burdens of our children and let them go free. Give them once again the literacy that made us the preeminent nation that we once were. No nation can afford to be powerful and illiterate too. America may have many faults, but it is still the greatest country on earth, and besides, it is the only country we have.

Let us once again return the teaching of the classics and poetry to our children. Let us once again set our children adrift in a sea of morality, and then the Iran incidents will not teach our children to believe in the noble lie that Plato talks of in his republic. Let us now begin to cease enunciating our principles and expressing our hopes, and become people of action. Let us begin to make our schools beacons of hope, not dens of dope and distribution centers for birth control pills. Rather than dealing with instant solutions for our children, let us find out why they behave the way they do. Could it be that we have allowed them to grow up without direction, without morals? Without attempting to help them arrange the puzzles of their minds? Without giving them heros and heroines to believe in? Is their definition of a hero just a sandwich?

As a fellow American, I beg each of you to once again relight the candles of excellence in America. Let us once again make the schools our children's workshops where they will come to believe that they are the source of progress, the parents of determination, and the origin of inspiration. Let us once again teach our children to tell time as well as purchase digital watches for them. Let us once again teach our children to tie their shoelaces as well as provide velcro closures for them. Let us once again teach our children the multiplication tables before we buy them calculators. Let us once again teach our children that the mind is the best computer before we put them on computers. Let us once again teach our children that difficult does not mean impossible, and that we see obstacles only when we lose sight of the goal of life.

Let us never have to answer our children's questions: "Where were you?" "How did America get in such bad shape?" Let each of us unlock our long-locked rusty hearts and make America the thundering great country that it can be, that it was, and let us once again listen together as the bells of liberty ring, knowing that it rings for each of us. What a wonderful legacy. What a privilege. Besides, do we really have a choice?

8

My Fight Not to Be a Part of the Real World

Nostalgically thinking, there once was a time when it was considered an insult when someone said, "You are not of this world," or "You are not a part of the real world." Today, I am easily offended when someone suggests that I become a part of the real world. And so, yes, yesterday's fact can become today's myth.

For the last decade or so, I have tumultuously struggled for my own identity. I have vehemently struggled not to become a part of the herd-instinct, or the issue-a-week-society that seems to do anything that feels good, looks good, or seems good.

The real world today seemingly consists of people who have ceased being human. They have become hollow people who know neither victory nor defeat. They are people who chase ascetically those things that they feels will bring them instant gratification, instant fame, or instant wealth.

There was a time when real doctors cared about real people. There was a time when real teachers declared that they would not allow their students to fail. There was a time when real people could not afford to turn their backs on the homeless, the poor, the disenfranchised, or the powerless. Today, in the real world, we have become inhumane enough to walk through life with a "So what? It's not my problem" attitude, a nonchalant turnstile attitude that ignores the I/Thou's principle.

I see so many people who declare, "What will happen to me if I become involved?" I see things that should not be, and I declare, like the Good Samaritan, "What will happen to these people if I do not become involved?" When we no longer become involved in the problems we attempt to solve, we then become robots held together by cold and callous bolts.

Thousands of visitors to our school often ask the question, "What do you do with children who must return to such fetid homes?" I often wonder whether, if these negative citizens of modernity had lived during the time of Abraham Lincoln, they would have asked such an inane question. If so, Abe Lincoln, at the age of fourteen, ragged, lean, and still unable to read, would never have had the opportunity to become President of the United States. Surely some negative doomsday crier would have seen to it that he was placed in a learning disabled room, and his school records would have become ink-blotted with statistics. His soul would have been Stanined and measured until he, too, would have become the victim of someone's negative prediction. How many of us are Nostradamian enough to look into the seeds of time and decide which seed will grow, and which will not grow?

The real world tells us what we want to hear. The real world today seems to thrive on how much we earn and how much we take, and not how much we give back to others. The real world today seems to measure us by where we live, where we shop, where we travel, and how many "things" we possess. Meanwhile, it seems to me that Thoreau was right when he said the mass of men lead lives of quiet desperation. We are so determined to prove the "Me" in each of us that we have forgotten how to be human in extending some of the egotistical Me into the "Thou." We have forgotten the lessons of John Donne who warned us that none of us are an island unto ourselves, and that each of us is a piece of the continent and the failure of some of us diminishes the total worth of all of us.

9.

The Ignorant Perfection of Ordinary People

Today we hear the doomsday cries about the rising underclass in the fetid inner-cities of America. We hear the clamor of poor schools and school reform. We hear that more and more professors in colleges are now too busy with research to bother with teaching. Teacher strikes, teacher cut-backs, teacher apathy, lowered test scores, and just recently being called A Nation at Risk are enough to raise the hackles of even the most nonchalant turnstile citizen.

If we stop to think for a moment and remember our history, we will readily recall that it was the Harriet Tubmans who never learned to read or write and yet led the most historical freedom odyssey for slaves ever recorded. It was the slaves who learned to read by scribbling alphabets in the sand, who defied the tyrannical slave-owner's decree that no slave should learn to read or write.

These are the best of times, and the worst of times. It has always been citizens with the determination of a lit firecracker that have made the worst of times the best of times. Dickensianly speaking, society is no worse today than it has ever been. What has always made the fetid times in society better times were citizens who did not sit back with a "So-what-it's-not-my-problem-attitude." It was those determined citizens that picked away at the roots of evil rather than hacking away at the leaves of mediocrity.

Every doomsday cry on national television telling poor people that they are underclass, poor, depraved, and helpless only helps reinforce the "I am not responsible for what I do; poverty gives me license to be mediocre and a leaning failure in society." We can either use poverty and callous-ness as a stepping stone or a stumbling block. As Milton told us, "The mind can make a Heaven out of Hell, or a Hell out of Heaven."

Here, at Westside Preparatory School, we teach our children and our parents that we must always seek to be our own creators. We realize that second-handers always end up in the tiger's mouth. We realize that there are no free rides to freedom. We realize that freedom and self-esteem are never comfortable, and that he or she who wants to be free and comfortable does not deserve either. We teach our children and our parents to go down roads armed with their own vision, and not the vision of some study, and not to succumb to the statistics that get figures written at the ex-pense of our failure.

We teach our children at Westside Preparatory School that, although we have been taught that giving is a virtue, we cannot distribute until we have created. We believe that true Ayn Rand-like freedom means, "Hands Off." We believe that true freedom comes from individuals who are deter-mined to be self-generated, self-motivated, self-propelled. We believe that kites still fly highest with the winds at their backs. Right now the winds are quite turbulent in the inner-city, but we teach that this turbulence comes from the artifi-cial help of the government who gave people a fish but never bothered teaching them how to fish. In other words, the inner-cities never could have become so blighted without the government's help. Creation died unborn in America's inner-cities, and the people are now dying from a malady called the Second-Hander's Syndrome. As Ayn Rand so vividly states, "We cannot digest a meal in a collective stomach," and so it is. All men and women must create their own meals to be digested in their own individual stomachs.

Ordinary people must be taught that they too can aim for perfection. Ordinary people must be taught that Jesus Christ himself never attended a university or lived in an opulent home; nor do we read anywhere where Jesus asked those desirous of his help to write proposals justifying their need of his help. In other words, Jesus was an ordinary person doing extraordinary things.

Abraham Lincoln, according to history, did not learn to read until he was fourteen years of age. Again, we have an ordinary person rising to extraordinary heights.

Helen Keller, born blind, perhaps saw more than many seeing people. She refused, with the help of a determined teacher, Anne Sullivan, to let her handicap be a stumbling block. Perhaps one of the greatest assets of these people who turned the lemons of life into lemonade was that they did not have a bastion of zeitgeists around them telling them what they could not do. They did not have people around them justifying their handicaps. They therefore used their handicaps as assets, rather than liabilities.

We tell our students at Westside Preparatory School that they are better than other people. Better meaning that they are too good to fail. Better meaning that they must use the lemons of today to make lemonade for the future. Better meaning that they use the fetidness of today to make a glorious tomorrow. Better meaning that we will do it ourselves, and we refuse to have others design life's circles for us. In other words, better means that we will screw our courage to the sticking point, and we will not fail. We believe that failure is just as easy to combat as it is to accept. We realize with the clearest clarity that although education is difficult, we emphatically cannot afford the paths of failure. We realize without hesitation that the primrose paths of life always lead to a nasty place. We therefore believe that the American dream is filled with the ingredients mixed thoroughly by ordinary people who feared the American nightmare so deeply that, in their ignorance, they dared to explore and make possible the American dream. Each of us benefits today from the seeds planted by those ignorant people who dared to do extraordinary things. Their ignorance hurt so much that they dared to say, "We are not in the darkness; we are determined to find a light."

Together the Have-Nots in our society must begin to face the stark reality that we have lost our wisdom when we cannot admit our ignorance. The ignorance that I truly deplore is the failure to realize that no one will undo the heavy burdens of failure but those who must carry that burden daily. The weight of failure and mediocrity can be solved only by those who must carry this burden.

Freedom has never meant not being a slave; it is the memory of what slavery was like. Once this memory is indelibly engraved in our psyches, we will never once again return to the inhumanity of slavery. If we forget the whips and scorns of the past, we are bound to repeat the folly. Let us together remember what slavery was like so that we will use our ignorance to become perfectionists in self-determination and self-generation.

Robert Bruce watched the determination of a spider and decided that, if a spider could patiently weave strand by strand until a perfect web occurred, he would go out again to win a battle for Scotland.

Michelangelo could see a piece of marble in the streets of Florence, Italy, and declare, "Inside that piece of marble is an angel just dying to get out." He later carved magnificent pieces from marble that others saw as just that. . .marble. Michelangelo had vision, and the Bible tells us, "People without vision perish." Let us, then, envision that our vision of perfection can begin with our ignorance. Let us use our ignorance to find a light.

If Edison could try over two hundred times to perfect the light bulb and declare, "I now know that there are 200 ways not to make the light bulb," we then can decide from our failure that we now know how not to fail. Let us use this as a stepping stone to success rather than lying in our abysmal pit of failure waiting for some Good Samaritan to pull us out. What if we meet one of those Samaritans who may say, "But, what will happen to me if I stop to help this person?" We instead must ask, "What will happen to me if I do not help myself?"

Just as the teapot whistles when the tea is ready, we as people must now whistle quite loudly, "I am ready to accept the challenges for my own life." And the trip of success is one of challenge, never problems. We as a people have been patient with our failure. The "teapot" now whistles and calls us by name. Let us hear that call. We cannot hear the call if we are too intoxicated on drugs, or drunk with the wine of failure to pay attention. When the call comes, we must be prepared to act.

Let the ignorant masses in the inner-cities of America hear the clarion call. Let the ignorant and failing masses declare that enough is too much. Let us remove ourselves from our decadent past and declare loudly enough for the distant drums of the universe to hear that we the failing and ignorant masses will begin our odyssey to seek perfection borne of our ignorance. What a wonderful challenge. What a glorious legacy. Let us together seize the future by changing today.

10.
Smiling Through My Tears

We all have preconceived myths about what we think things are. The reality of what things really are seldom become universal truth.

Westside Preparatory School became somewhat of an enigma in an era when far too many inner-city children were left out of the American dream. The streets, crime, and other decadent factors in our society beckoned far too many of them, welcoming them to the Stony-Hearted Main Streets of society. The American dream of becoming doctors, scientists, lawyers, candlestick makers became an illusive process for them. Usually by the time the average inner-city child even hears of college, they have failed far too miserably to even consider college, and so a lifetime of failure becomes the manacles that withhold their souls from progress and self-esteem.

In order to combat just a few of the miserable statistics concerning black children, I started Westside Preparatory School on the second floor of my home in September, 1975. After fourteen years in the local public school, it became painfully obvious that education was not meant for our children. Most of the children attending the Delano Elementary School were considered "losers" by the system, "failures" in their own eyes after repeated doses of "You-will-never-amount-to-very-much," federal funds that actually paid for their failure, and nonchalant turnstile attitudes of non-caring and callous teachers protected by a powerful union, weak administrators, and unknowing parents. The system, therefore, became a self-perpetuating hierarchy bent on perpetuating more and more illiterates isometrical to the parents before them.

After fourteen years of frustration, tears, and peer isolation, I decided that I could no longer expect things to change for the better in a system that recruited children only for the worst.

With five thousand dollars in pension funds, carpentry skill from my husband and support from my family, Westside Preparatory School was born out of desperation and a determination to make just a few children's lives better.

A one-room school in a large inner-city where architects' dreams in the way of buildings can be a rare oddity. Soon the *Chicago Sun-Times* did a feature article of some of the children's writings in their paper, and then *People* did an article, then the *Chicago Tribune*, and a few local television stations, and soon a call came from *60 Minutes*. Children learning in a one-room school ambience was great copy. I have a personal saying about *60 Minutes*: If one gets through the research and rudiments of *60 Minutes,* he should be able to walk into Heaven with no problems.

I understand, from a letter written to us by *60 Minutes*, that the segment called "Marva" drew more viewer response than any other segment. Black children reading and understanding Dante, Chaucer, Tolstoy, Nietzsche, Dostoevski, Emerson, Milton, Shakespeare, Faulkner, Jung, Wilkie Collins, Hume, Socrates, Plato, and Aristotle awakened many long-locked rusty hearts in America who too long have assumed that inner-city children could not learn.

As with any enterprise, if the product is average, it will be left severely alone; however, if it becomes a masterpiece, it will set a million tongues a-wagging. And so it was with Westside Preparatory School. The critics' fork-tongued criticism and envy and hate soon brought a ton of bricks down on my head. The same school that has been lauded and praised in so many television programs and articles became a target for the shafts of critics and naysayers. The movie *The Marva Collins Story*, starring Cicely Tyson as a caring and dedicated teacher, did not set well with many public school teachers who insisted that our children should continue to go into society wearing the scars and mistakes generic to the inner-city. How dare anyone declare that all children could achieve if they were not taught too thoroughly that they could not achieve?

I had finally escaped the feeling of being in alien-camp at my former public school. I had finally left the cruel mood of teachers not talking to me, of receiving the unsigned hate notes, but I had not escaped the hate that would follow me—yes, even to yelling loud and long that I was a fake! Even the sheltered walls of my home would not help me escape the sea of hate I had left in the public system and all because I cared. . .about our children.

In reality, every time I saved a child who had been written off in the public school system, or saved a child who had been measured, ink-blotted and Stanined into failure, I made another enemy. Every time I made a "lifter" out of a potential "leaner," I only created more animosity. Every time I made a child feel good about himself and his world, I created a label of being "controversial and a liar." The price and membership fees in the Club of Caring is very expensive, and now I know why the membership is so exclusive and the members are so few.

After the movie *The Marva Collins Story* was filmed, I decided to purchase a larger building for our growing enrollment. I found even more difficulties. No one would sell me a building, or the price became so great that I could not afford it. Without much choice, I purchased two factory buildings and had them renovated to classrooms.

Knowledge is like an electrical generator. Somehow the eyes light up like Fort Knox when the ray of knowledge takes over illiteracy. Self-esteem soars, self-determination takes on a new speed, and, most of all, the self-perpetuating hierarchy of failure dies unborn.

Some of the records of the children were unbelievable. It seemed that many of the teachers of these children had spent more time getting things "written" on the children's records than they had in getting the lives of the children "right." The records were unbelievable in that all of the things that the former records indicated that the children could not do, they were able to do. With support, determination, and faith in the potential of these children, many of them scored three and four grade levels beyond their entering scores. Most of all, these children had learned to turn the lackluster light in their eyes into a ray of radiance, and self-esteem was once again their very own.

Perhaps the most poignant situation of inner-city children is that their parents, too, finally believe that they are worthless. The teachers either passively let them know that they are not champions worth wrestling with, or they directly tell them so, and then the child finds no solace at home, and school becomes, also, a dreaded nightmare. The streets then become their friend, their only friend that accepts them without negative superlatives. For once in their lives, they find that they can do something right. . .destroy the world in a bath of hate, and sadly, they also destroy themselves, and once again society becomes the hated target. Hope for these children becomes a carpet of glass, and dreams are yesterday's irretrievable ashes. These children become a platform for more and more studies and politicians' enunciated hopes and expressed principles that land them votes and a reason for campaigning. The public schools in turn use the fetid statistics compiled about these children to anchor themselves on more and more excuses as to why they do such a poor job of educating the children. In other words, it becomes a vicious circle that is self-perpetuating, and, of course, the poor become a profitable commodity to be traded and sold to the highest bidder. That bidder is usually the federal government, who actually helped to miseducate so many children. Educators never could have done such a miserable job alone.

11.
The Comprachicos

Ayn Rand wrote a very revealing article called "The Comprachicos." The Comprachicos, or comprapequenos, were a strange and hideous nomadic association famous in the seventeenth century, forgotten in the eighteenth century, unknown today.

Comprachicos, as well as *comprapequenous,* is a compound Spanish word that means "child-buyers." The comprachicos traded in children. They bought them and sold them. And what did they make of these children? Monsters. Why monsters? To make people laugh. The people need laughter; so did kings. Cities required side-show freaks or clowns; palaces required jesters. To succeed in producing a freak, one must get hold of him early. A dwarf must be started when he is small. . .

Hence an art. There were educators. They took a man and turned him into a miscarriage; they took a face and made a muzzle. They stunted growth; they mangled features. Where God had put a straight glance, this art of miseducation put a squint. Where God had put harmony, they put deformity. Where God had put perfection, they brought back a botched attempt. And in the eyes of society it was the botched that was perfect. . .

In China, since time immemorial, they had achieved refinement in a special art and industry: the molding of a living man. One takes a child two or three years old, one puts him into a porcelain vase, more or less grotesque in shape, without cover or bottom, so that the head and feet protrude. In the day time, one keeps this vase standing upright; at night, one lays it down, so that the child can sleep. Thus the child expands without growing, slowly filling the contours of the vase with his compressed flesh and twisted bones. This bottled development continues for several years. At a certain point, it becomes irreparable. When one judges that this has occurred and that the monster is made, one breaks the vase, the child comes out, and one has a man in the shape of a pot. (From Victor Hugo, *The Man Who Laughs*.)

The Comprachicos today are educators in modernity. They put a child into a mold, they create the herd-instinct mentality, they ink-blot, measure, test and Stanine until the child finds that finding the real self becomes an illusive process. Today the stealing of a child is done in the open; only the results are hidden. The operation is done in the open; the scars strip one of self-esteem and self-determination. The stony-hearted cold streets welcome, beckoning these children to come as they are, no questions asked. These children are never taught to read, write, compute, or reason, and we all know that once we teach men to hate reason they will automatically hate themselves.

The Chinese vase-molding is no longer in vogue today, but the molding still prevails. The molding today is done in the seats of the average American classroom with teachers paid by taxpayers. The normal development of every "miracle" that enters the American classroom is almost assured of failure and mediocrity. The child who questions, queries and thinks for himself is soon recruited to become a part of the "herd-mentality." Just fill in the blanks, copy from the blackboards, sit quietly and militaristically in rows of orderly seats and develop a robotized mentality, and you are a good student. The child who is self-motivated becomes teacher-motivated. The child who is self-propelled gets his wings clipped. The child who is self-generated gets his motor turned off. Children very soon learn to go along if they are ever to get along with the teacher. The self-perpetuating hierarchy of the Comprachicos works well, and society once again becomes deluged with another perennial crop of robotized non-thinkers.

To the caring teachers who may read this, I quote you a little food for thought taken from Ayn Rand's *Atlas Shrugged*:

> He thought of all the living species that train their young in the art of survival, the cats who teach their kittens to hunt, the birds who spend such strident effort on teaching their fledglings to fly—yet man, whose tool of survival is the mind, does not merely fail to teach a child to think, but devotes the child's education to the purpose of destroying his brain, of convincing him that thought is futile and evil, before he has started to think. . .
>
> Men would shudder, he thought, if they saw a mother bird plucking the feathers from the wings of her young, then pushing him out of the nest to struggle for survival. . .yet that was what they did to their children.
>
> Armed with nothing but meaningless phrases, this boy had been thrown to fight for existence, he had hobbled and groped through a brief doomed effort, he had screamed his indignant, bewildered protest. . .and had perished in his first attempt to soar on his mangled wings.

Let us no longer allow our children to attempt to fly with mangled wings. Let us give them wings that will allow them to fly to the highest heights.

12

The Designers of Human Failure

There was a time in our curriculums in American schools when virtue occupied center stage. There also was a time when children memorized poetry and had to tell what the moral lesson in that poem meant to them. Schools were actually the most hallowed chamber in the House of Intellect. Today we have clouded our schools with cobwebs and clutter that have sullied the appearance and clogged the machinery of the Academic world. The large objective of schools some time ago was to train the moral character and nourish the souls of the students. Any teacher took it personally if any student could not read, write, compute, and think critically and analytically.

Lessons were prefaced with Longfellow's poem, "Keeping His Word," and the lessons inherent in *The Pied Piper of Hamelin*, and what happens when we break a promise. Classics such as *Androcles and the Lion, The Fox and the Grapes, Aesop's Fables*, and selections from Emerson's *Self-Reliance*, and other great classics permeated the academic day. Today, American school children are served the banalities of seeing Sue and Jimmy running through the pages of a basal reader. If students succeed in guessing at the non-phonetic approach that teachers use to teach reading, they are then asked to answer a few simple questions at the end of the selection. Teacher-pupil dialogue and group discussion have taken a back seat to students guessing the answers to true and false questions and checking multiple choice questions.

We have done a very good job in creating more and more underachievers, and this, of course, accounts for the daily violence in our classrooms. Our children are what they are taught, just as we are all what we eat. Teach a student mediocrity, and we shall reap mediocrity. This does not take several million-dollar studies to tell us what we should know from no more than just common-sense.

Good literature, good poetry, and good thinking exercises are as rare in today's textbooks as seeing a dinosaur on the nearest freeway. Virtue today has fallen into disrepute.

The average college-educated teacher goes into the classroom armed with the same banalities taught him in grammar school and college, and so miseducation becomes a self-perpetuating hierarchy. About all we have left of traditional values is a little corner called tolerance.

In our issue-a-week-society, we have failed to teach our children the basics of telling time; we use digital watches. Children cannot tie shoelaces; we use velcro. Children do not memorize the multiplication tables today; they use calculators. They never learn the basics; we put them on computers. They do not write compositions today; they creatively check true and false questions and multiple choice questions. We have chipped away the walls of what we once knew as basics in the name of creativity. Judas Priest! Shouldn't one learn the basics before we become creative? Think momentarily of a creative surgeon that never learned the basics.

Teachers all across America realize that something is wrong in our schools, but many of them are too intimidated by the value-neutrality to speak out. Few of us can bring ourselves to say: "This is wrong. I will not be a part of this." During my fourteen years in the public schools, teachers would constantly hand me notes of questions to ask during a teachers' meeting because they were too intimidated to speak out. I soon learned that, by speaking out, I put myself in alien-camp to be despised and hated and called a troublemaker! Thoreau was right, however, when he said, "Men boil at different degrees." I could take no more of the hallowed mediocrity that actually paid teachers to recruit students to fail, and so, after fourteen years of battling for the rights of children, I became a public school drop-out.

We have taught flimsy standards of behavior in our schools, and then news article after news article writes about today's unruly students. We actually hire police guards to protect us from the very students we created.

Schools created a whole new lexicon for today's miseducated students. They are called At Risk Students, Learning Disabled, Mentally Educable Handicapped—the list is infinite. I call them the students of Teacher Inabilities, rather than learning disabilities.

Because we have ceased teaching moral values in our schools, we now find those same miseducated students are putting more and more mind-altering drugs into our society. Human greed and human ingenuity have found ways to get under, over, and around, and through, any barriers we erect because of the money available from the army of drug users. Just as we refused to say to our students, "I am sorry; you will not fail," we have found it seemingly impossible to say to anyone, "I am sorry, pot-smoking is unacceptable behavior, and you must not do it." The very thought, we are told, is subversive of liberty, civil rights, and personhood. And so, we find ourselves as a nation in the ludicrous and indefensible situation of putting heavy pressure on other governments to penalize their citizens for producing and exporting drugs when we will not penalize our own people for using them. You Mexicans and Columbians and Turks, you must crack down on your citizens who produce the drugs, but we refuse to make any serious effort to penalize our people for using them. I have seen teachers, administrators too, walk right by students who were exhibiting deviant behavior.

Our schools are bad because few of us are willing to go against what seems to be the standard of conduct that is accepted by many. This is why Emerson's lines from *Self-Reliance* are so important for our students to memorize: "He who would be a man must be a nonconformist." We must create more and more students and American adults who are not afraid of social stigma.

Pure scholarship purged of every other moral concern is, in my opinion, dangerous scholarship. We must never forget what happened in Auschwitz. Were not the Germans scholarly? We must never forget what happens when scholarship prevails without the companionship of morality.

Recently, Secretary Bennett, our Secretary of Education (a job I was asked to take by President Reagan, but declined), said, "American education must return to morality." And, alarming as it may be, the President of one of our most prestigious universities, Princeton, said, "Mr. Bennett is an embarrassment to American education; we teach students how to think; not how to behave." One can think of ways to kill everyone over 60, too, but is this moral?

Many of our great institutions of learning of the past have embraced the research role that rejects moral education, scorning it as indoctrination; as terrorism of the mind. With this kind of attitude, we have therefore created terrorists of society. . .all created, paid for by the government, and made in our American schools. Few, if any, of our American institutions of higher learning have acknowledged, explained, and justified their transition to their constituencies or to the general public. What is perhaps saddest is that parents and taxpayers never noticed that our academic institutions have become such failures. Our children keep telling us that something is wrong, but their pleas and crimes and other means of telling us that they are hurting seem to ring hollow.

Our five- and four-year-olds today can memorize the Madison Avenue sales jingles, but, according to our educators, they cannot memorize a short poem, the multiplication tables, or what they learned in school for one day. Push-outs in our schools—I call them "push-outs" rather than "drop-outs"—can hot-wire a car and create all kinds of havoc, yet they cannot, according to our teachers, learn to do a detailed scientific experiment. What a waste of human potential!

We see parts of our creations in our adults. They are the new generation: the drop-outs. . .the pushed-outs. . .the "I don't care" generation. They are the antithesis of the Puritan culture, with its strict beliefs and control which founded our country. . .

They are our religious institutions that have mellowed their messages to make the homilies palatable to today's new generation.

They are the people who enter the job market with a "What's in it for me?" attitude, or a "How much can I get, and how little can I give?" attitude.

They are the transient couples that live together for a few months and then move on to another transient relationship. They are the people who have little regard for marriage as a ceremony or for vows of permanence. . .

They are the generation that is looking to be "turned on". . .they live in a state of perpetual boredom, and usually drugs, alcohol, pills, or racy relationships are the buzz words for them.

They are the generation that has little respect for the work ethics of the past. . .they do not think of the future; they live for now.

They are the generation that does not worry about what history will say of them; they live from moment to moment. This kind of do-your-own-thing generation was home grown in our American schools and tolerated by changing family attitudes. Family attitudes that were afraid to hang on to what worked for them as parents, and teachers who tossed out the old in favor of the untried new thing of the day. In other words, we threw the old morality on the garbage heap and developed our own set of moral standards, and the Ten Commandments became known as the ten suggestions.

Our textbooks allowed our children to develop their own relevant feelings, their own ideas, their own morality standards and their own beliefs, and, capriciously, our children destroyed themselves in a bath of hate and ignorance, unrestrained by former moral standards.

While Sidney Simon, the Values Clarification supporter, was busy filling our classrooms with materials that taught them that it was okay to do that which felt good, most parents did not even realize that their children's minds were being used as guinea pigs in tax-supported schools. The irony of this is that we tell our children to just say No to drugs, and on the other hand we have told them to do anything that feels good. Is there little wonder our children are confused?

Schools ceased preparing citizens to become responsible citizens and began teaching them to become fulfilled citizens who obtained their personal needs and material success at any cost. We have had a reversal of the wisdom of the ages. Today, we have taught our children no beliefs and no faith. Is that the goal of a true education?

Apparently we have changed the Ten Commandments to suit our own purpose; have we also juxtaposed the words of Jesus to say, "You shall know doubt and doubt shall set you free"? Our greatest intellectual aim today seems to be intellectual clever debunking. The fellow that can convince the greatest number of people of the greatest lie, and do it in a clever and artistic way, seems to hold the reins for leadership.

Didn't we learn any lesson from doing our own thing when the plague of AIDS entered our society? Didn't we learn a lesson from doing our own thing when drugs became the Hydra-headed monster of our time? Didn't we learn anything from a do-your-own-thing society when we rejected basic education and became so creative and new in our approach to education that we are now called a Nation at Risk? Didn't we learn anything when, as a government, we spent monies that we did not have, and we now have more global debt than our heirs will be able to pay?

The rediscovery and affirmation of substantive values is, of course, a large, complex, and sensitive task, easier to enunciate than to accomplish, and we are without guidance for the undertaking. Few people are willing to brave the censure of their colleagues, the wrath of society, the scorn of the critics to say, "Enough is too much." The few individuals today who declare that we are a nation in decline often find themselves in alien-camp, and they become a bit battle-fatigued, and so they too join the journey into oblivion.

That segment of our society that served as the bellwethers which led the American culture out into the seductive, but dangerous, territory of absolute openness and non-judgmentalness must now pull in the reins for the rest of us; we all must come home again. . .home again to the standards that made us a great nation in the first place. We must begin to set guidelines for acceptable conduct and remove the infinite do-your-own-thing attitude. Together, we must once again decide what is acceptable, decent, desirable, and our children must not be allowed to receive these judgments from the national glare of television.

Should America continue its present odyssey into decadence, then we are saying that there is nothing left in our society to safeguard. We are saying that there is nothing worthy of celebrating. We are saying that we are not concerned about the kind of world we leave our generic heirs.

I end with the words of Isaiah from the Bible: "Undo the heavy burdens cast upon our children, and let them go free.". . .free to lead moral lives. . .free to lead us into safety because we made today morally better so that there would be a tomorrow for all of us. To do less than this is truly a sin of omission.

13

A Society is What
We Teach Our Children

Shakespeare said: "Some men are born great, some achieve greatness, and others have greatness thrust upon them." I believe that all teachers have the capacity and potential to become reformers. All of us who take the Latin meaning of the word *teacher* ("to lead or draw out") to heart, will, like Pygmalion, see in each child the opportunity to either curse what our children bring to us, or light their lives with our own illuminations.

We hear so much today about the demise of morals in our society, and I am awed by the things that shock society. I am amazed because we reap what we sow, and we have perennially sown bad seeds. Now that we reap bad fruit, we cry doomsday cries, lamenting about the poor crop of young people our society has created. Yet we, the adults, teachers, and parents, have watered and nurtured our present crop of amoral children.

Remember when each of us had to write daily: "Do unto others as you would have them do unto you"? If the rose-colored glasses will permit, think for a moment how many of us grew up on the lessons inherent in the *Pied Piper of Hamelin*. We learned that we must all pay the piper; terrible consequences will befall those who do not keep their promises. Today's generation has learned from our lack of teaching them morals that we promise the piper anything and then slay him if we later decide the price is too high.

Remember when we actually read aloud the lessons inherent in *Macbeth*? We learned to steer clear of the seven deadly sins that destroyed Macbeth. Today, if children learn anything at all about Macbeth, it is usually accomplished using prepackaged lesson plans which in no way challenge children to read well. Later, children will take an inane True or False test that allows them to guess at the correct answer. An oral discussion or oral reading of a selection has become pretty much like seeing a dinosaur on the expressway.

How many of our children today are exposed to Emerson's *Self-Reliance*? The words, "Trust thyself, every heart beats to that iron string" are alien to today's students.

How many of our children have been exposed to the myth of *Hercules and the Lazy Man*? As the man exhorts the gods' help, Hercules tells him to put his shoulder to the wheel and help himself. How many of our children have grown up today believing that success must be pursued for themselves? They have not been told that the pursuit for happiness must be their own undertaking.

We constantly speak of the lack of leaders in our country, and allegedly we have forgotten that Homer's Achilles, Shakespeare's Othello, Miller's Willy Loman are all people who have struggled with the same kinds of intractable, maddening leadership problems that face each of us every day. We can learn from their victories. . .and their defeats. Plato's *Republic* can teach more insight into leadership than any textbook I know. Plato himself was a down-to-earth, hands-on leader with a proven track record of successful innovation. What we talk about today as hands-on management was practiced by Plato thousands of years ago. Plato knew that leadership hinged on asking the right questions. He asked these questions orally and did not have students guessing at true and false answers.

John Ruskin wrote, "All books could be divided into two classes: the books of the hour and the books of all time." It would seem to me that the books of all time would be those great books and great ideas that produce great citizens. There is an old adage that states, "Great oaks grow from little acorns." This is as true today as when it was first muttered. We cannot expect to reap shade amidst rotten acorns. The fruit does not fall far from the tree on which it was borne. If our children are amoral, they are as they are because we did not teach them morals.

Someone said that today's generation actually believes that Moses brought down ten suggestions from Mount Sinai. As I lecture across the country, helping other school districts seek better ways of educating their children, I actually asked 2,000 children in numerous cities if they knew the difference between the Ten Commandments and the Ten Suggestions. Only 12 out of 2,000 children had ever heard of the Ten Commandments. Only 8 out of that 2,000 knew the Ten Commandments. Judas Priest! How can we expect moral behavior from our children when they never learned right from wrong in the first place?

In the name of relevance, today's generation actually had immorality thrust upon them. How did we ever expect our children to learn morality from seeing Dick and Jane running through the pages of the readers of the day? Poetry such as Kipling's *If*, which implores young people to live through the best and worst times alike, is replaced with such nonsensical, cutesy, rhyming poetry that teaches children little of nothing. Poetry such as *The House by the Side of the Road* teaches children that we are all a piece of a single whole, and that we have a duty to each other as a member of the family of Man.

When inner-city children were not learning to read, few of us said anything. It was not our children, so it did not concern us. When drugs were used solely by inner-city residents, few of us were overly concerned. When hideous crimes were committed by inner-city children, we thought "Thank God we live away from the city."

Now that the blight that once affected only inner-city children has become the rich man's malady too, there is no choice anymore. We all must speak up, or perish as the perfect complacents of our time. If this does not inspire us to act, then we must realistically ask ourselves the consequences of being led by an amoral generation. Either each of us must do what we can to relight the flickering candles of morality in our society or we all shall be forced to grope in the darkness.

If none of the above frightens us into action, we must then remember the lessons of history. Remember the greatness of Rome? Remember how all roads once led to Rome? Remember how they too, thought that good meant forever? Rome crumbled, did it not? Is this to become our fate?

14.
All's Well That Ends Well

Think for a moment — Abraham Lincoln was fourteen years of age before he learned to read. By today's standards, he probably would have been placed in a learning disabled class and never had the opportunity to become President of the United States.

Einstein was often accused of daydreaming in the classroom. The teacher never bothered to discover that he was trying to determine the radius of the shadows that came through his classroom window.

It is said that Edison tried over two hundred times to develop the light bulb and finally declared, "At least I now know how not to do it." Each of these people used stumbling blocks as stepping stones. Each of these individuals turned lemons into lemonade. Can't we, too, do that with our students?

The girl in seat seven in the first row once missed one hundred days of a one-hundred-eighty-five school day year. Today she is here with her dirty dress on the wrong side because she did not want to miss school. This year, for the very first time, Joan has not missed a day of school. The teacher validates her, and wherever we find validation, we succeed.

The boy in seat three in the first row has never had the opportunity to sit near the front. Every teacher before him has always put him in the back of the room. Few teachers have ever believed in him. Few teachers could ever see beyond the veneer of "I don't care" and change that to, "I am accepted." The teacher validates him, and wherever we find validation, we succeed.

The girl in seat six, row four has never been touched unless she was being punished for something. The daily hugs and praises now let her know that she is worthy of love and acceptance. The old perfume bottles filled with water that she gifts me with daily is her way of saying, "Thank you for loving me." The teacher validates her, and wherever we find validation, we succeed.

When children succeed, the teacher succeeds. When the teacher succeeds, the world succeeds. When the world succeeds, we find peace. Where we find peace, we find love. Where there is love, all things are possible.

15.
The Purpose of an Education

An education may do many things for you, if you are made of the right stuff, for you cannot fasten a two-thousand dollar education to a fifty-cent boy. The fool, the dude, and the shirk come out of school still not knowing anything, and they actually come out of the school pretty much as they went in. They dive deep in the Pierian Springs (whoever quaffed of these waters were supposed to be inspired by the Muses). As the duck who lives in the pond, they come up dry as the duck does. The school will not do anything for you if you do not wish to do something for yourself; but a well-spent life in school is one of the greatest helps to all good things.

So if you learn to use it rightly, this an education do for you: It will bring you in contact with the great minds of the past, the long roll of those who, through the ages, have borne a mission to young men and young women, from Plato to Emerson, from Homer and Euripides to Schiller and Browning. Your thought will be limited not by the narrow gossip of today, but the great men of all ages, and all climes will become your brothers. You will learn to feel what the Greek called the "consolations of philosophy"; you will walk with Socrates as he walks through the streets of Athens, saying "I know nothing, or I am not Greek, I am not Athenian, I am a citizen of the world." To turn from the petty troubles of the day to the thoughts of the masters, to go from the noise of the dingy street through the door of a cathedral. If you learn to unlock those portals, no power on earth can take from you the key. The whole of your life must be spent in your own company; school will help you like yourself. The uneducated man is like a leaf blown from here to there believing whatever he is told; the educated man finds his own way. An education will bring you face to face with the great problems of nature. You will learn from nature's lava laws, more than the books can tell you, of the grandeur, the power, the omnipotence of God. You will learn to face great problems seriously. You will learn to work patiently at their solution, though you know that many generations must each add its mite to your work before any answer can be reached. You, the educated man, will learn to become a lifter and not a leaner; you will not always seek the easy way but will find the hardest way alone without crying, without complaining. You will lift loads thinking that it is God's gift.

The educated man does not have the time to be mean. He learns to work patiently, and he builds for future generations to come by planting the trees today so that his generic heirs may receive the shade.

The ideal child in school is not cheap, mean, cruel or unkind and is much like *David Copperfield's* Agnes, "always pointing the way upward."

This we all are if we have teachers who give of their love and not of their thoughts; who let us create rather than emulate; who let us look within ourselves rather than to their thoughts, realizing that we will create our own if given an opportunity.

The educated man is never selfish or pedantic, showing his learning for learning's sake; he uses it to help others who may fall by the wayside without his help. The educated man carries a candle, ready to ignite another pilgrim's flickering lamp.

To know a good teacher is indeed a blessing. That teacher should be repaid—with your giving to another person as that teacher has given to you. This is the greatest repayment any teacher could possibly have.

The good student leaves school better prepared than when he went in. The good student is there for a purpose, and you will never waste time by associating with him. Among the truly educated are the best young men and women of the times. They mold each other's character and shape each other's work. Many a student will tell you that above all else which school gave was the values of friendship. Value your friends; they are rare!

Again, school intensifies the individuality of a man. It takes his best abilities and raises him to the second, or third, or tenth power, as we say in mathematics. It is true enough that schools try to make students conform to being less of an individual—to cast all students in the same mold. The good school does not place readiness above thoroughness, memory above mastery, glibness above sincerity, uniformity above originality, and the rules and modes of the dead past above the work of the living present.

But say what you will of old methods, they often attained great ends: schools have aimed at uniformity. They did not secure it. The individuality of the student bursts through the cast-iron curriculum. A man becomes what nature meant him to be, because he has a trained mind to think for himself.

The educated person has the courage of his conviction because only he has any real convictions of his own. He knows how convictions should be formed. What he believes he takes on his own evidence—not because it is the creed of his time, or the belief of his peers. To see things as they really are is one of the crowning privileges of the educated man, and to help others to see them so is one of the greatest services he can render to society. As Theodore Roosevelt said in his essay "The American Boy," "Life is a football game. Hit the line hard; don't foul and don't shirk, but hit the line hard."

16.

A Fable

Once upon a time there was a little red hen who decided that the schools of her time were indeed bad, so she decided to start her own school. She figured that surely she could not do any worse than the academicians of her time. She called the Cat and she said, "Who will help me start a school?"

"Not I," said the Cat. "It is not my problem. Besides, the parents do not care about their children, so why should I bother?"

She called the Dog, and she said, "Dog, Dog, will you help me start a school so that our children may dare to have a better education?"

"No," said the Dog, "I have too much to do and, besides, one cannot change the bureaucratic system of failure."

So she called the Pig. She said, "Pig, Pig, will you help me start a school?"

"No," said the Pig. "Besides, why bother to teach this generation anything? They are all drug-crazed and wild."

So she called the Rat, and she said, "Rat, Rat, will you help me start a school so that our children may dare to feel good about themselves and their world again?"

"No," said the Rat. "Education was only meant to take a few people to great and lasting heights, and, besides, these animals will never be more than what they are anyway, so why bother?"

"Well," said the Little Red Hen, "they will never more than what they are if we DO NOT BOTHER, so I will do it myself." And she did.

The Little Red Hen took a corner of the barnyard and cleaned it very thoroughly. All of the animals, of course, laughed at her make-shift school. After all, the rest of the animals all enjoyed well-constructed and well-lit buildings with all of the equipment one could possibly think of. Their school was well-funded, and well-supplied. Meanwhile, the pupils of the Little Red Hen had to scratch their numerals in the sand of the barnyard, and they had to count the grains of corn instead of having the fancy computers of their peers. The Little Red Hen, however, felt not one moment of chagrin, for she knew that her efforts were worth it—if she only saved her own baby chicks. Soon, however, the animals of the Little Red Hen's school began to do very well. They soon discovered that it was the "things" that their friends had in school that prevented them from learning. They soon discovered that the monies and the funding actually paid for more and more animals to be placed in learning disabled rooms. The Little Red Hen and her pupils benefited from the cast-away books that the other school systems declared too difficult for their pupils to read. They also benefited from the innate tools that all animals have— the ability to use their brains, and not "things." She soon discovered that "things" do not teach; animals do. She soon discovered that the mandarins of the educational establishment did not themselves know how to educate animals, since the only way they knew to solve a problem was to do more and more animal studies and to throw more and more federal dollars at the problem. She found out that only hard work and determination and, yes, a love for her pupils truly get results.

Soon, reporters from all over the world started to appear in the barnyard and call her work a miracle. You see, the animals of her time did not understand common sense and hard work. They only understood the use of "things" and more and more federal dollars. They only understood making more and more excuses for failure. They called her work a Back-to-Basics program. She had not gone BACK to anything. She simply believed all the time that all animals could learn if they were not taught too thoroughly that they couldn't learn.

Since the Little Red Hen didn't have free time to write more and more negative reports about her students, she therefore had more time to work with her students, and, rather than get reports written, she spent more time getting things "right." She had no federal forms to fill out, and, therefore, she could spend this time too getting the lives of the animals right.

Since bad education seemed at the time a blight that would not go away, soon the accolades for the Little Red Hen's work made the establishment very angry, and a ton of bricks were dropped on her head from the powers that benefited from poor education. The Little Red Hen was accused of attempting to overthrow the public school system. As state institutions, the public schools of her time were well protected from the forces that normally determine the success or failure of a private enterprise. Monopolies flourish in the public sector because of its hierarchical bureaucratic structure which rewards conformity and discourages competition. Those who work their way up to positions of power and control in the hierarchy use that power by way of tenure to solidify and perpetuate their control, and they were not about to be ridiculed by a little barnyard school that was a David against a Goliath. In other words, they were not about to be ridiculed by one Little Red Hen against a system that was self-perpetuating. The establishment meant to continue their orgy of spending and hiring more and more teachers to fail students. This, too, of course, made a joyful noise among suppliers and easy-to-read, easy-to-teach publishers. This also brought new prosperity for the establishment and untold sorrow and failure for more and more animals.

As long as the Little Red Hen did not produce a threat to the system, she was a commodity of ridicule. However, once results occurred, the agents and keepers of failure in America began to harass her. The building inspectors began to pay unmitigated calls. Teachers and the mandarins of education began to criticize her. Free enterprise is fine and welcomed in America, but do not use it to attempt to educate thinking animals.

The rapaciousness of the system was being challenged by

one Little Red Hen, and, of course, the experts with all of the answers all of the time and humanity for the animals none of the time were not about to sit this one out without a battle. The callous aristocracies of history were not about to loose the rein of failing children; after all, schools were never meant to serve children—they were established to perpetuate the bureaucrats that are rhetorical rather than teach. The puffed-up peacocks of the educational establishment with egos of majestic proportions were not about to be told they were doing it all WRONG! The DOLLARS spent on education were going to be heard, and anybody attempting to disdain this would be punished and sent to the corner to redeem their sins of ever attempting to speak for the animal children.

The former grandiloquent compliments regarding the Little Red Hen's work was to be discredited, and that had to be done immediately. The establishment, therefore, quickly thought of a smear campaign that would prove to all of the Barnyard society that they were right all the time. After all, lowered SAT scores and lowered reading scores only required more and more dollars in order to get the scores higher. Anybody saying that these things were not needed would not be tolerated.

The twenty-three million illiterates in the Barnyard society and the thirty-five million functional illiterates and the two million illiterates being added to that figure each year surely needed more federal dollars so more and more illiterates could be recruited, and we, of course, could continually be labeled a Nation at Risk, a nation crumbling deliberately. The bloated vessels of the educational establishment reeling under the weight of their own self-importance was not about to become charitable toward the barnyard animals. The idolatry of bowing to power became an incurable and self-induced disease, and it was not to be challenged or questioned.

The Little Red Hen, however, realized that animals yield very painfully to change. She also rationalized that whenever one comes to drain the swamps they must be cognizant of the crocodiles, but they must never sit on the shores and cry crocodile tears. She saw the problems of the animals of her time, and, notwithstanding the dangers and criticism of her colleagues and the disdain of society, she was determined to oppose the foes of her time to insure our children the right to breathe literacy.

The Little Red Hen continues her plight, often in isolation; but the wonder of the animals' eyes holding wonder like a cup is more than enough reward to make up for the wrath of the establishment.

MORAL: It is easier to Stanine, ink-blot, and measure children's failure than it is to prove that all children can learn if they are never taught too thoroughly that they were born to fail. Things and architects' dream buildings do not teach; animals do.

17

January Sixth, Nineteen Eighty-One

Dearest Children of Westside Preparatory School:

To say "I love you" would be inadequate, to show you that I love you is indeed the hardest task of all. I feel unappreciated by people, but I know all the time that you, the children, our future, my future, my world, our America, depends on what you do here today, or. . .there will be no tomorrow for any of us.

As you all know, I have been offered one job after another in high places, but it is for you, the children who sit here today, who tomorrow will bear the torch that will enlighten the world, that I remain here. It is for you alone that I continue to bear the struggles and toil of caring, the Herculean task of working when I should be resting. Yes, you children for whom I have stood at the blackboard dizzy with fatigue and yet, you, children, never knew that I thought each breath would be my last! It is for you that I spent a prayerful Saturday alone praying and asking God to guide me either to go to Washington or to remain in an area that everyone else has fled several comfortable eons away. I have emphatically taken the hardest task, the road seldom taken, but may that road make a difference in your lives, in your children's lives; most important, may one day we as a people reach the promised land that we gave ourselves because we learned here that it will not be given to us. May each of you never retreat and may you be heard! May you fire imaginations, plumb the ethers, chart your own futures, lead your own causes; and most of all may you always have your own thoughts. May those thoughts always point upwards for another brother who may have lost his way without your guidance, without your stick-to-it-iveness, without your determination, without your example—when everything except God overhead and your heart within, says "Turn back," you continue on." May you never seek the bubble reputation in a world made of cannons! Always, children, let truth and honesty drip from your lips even though there will be people with double determination coming to scoff what you do; if you continue to press forward, those same men will remain to sing your praises! People like to make you underdogs, but remember, people seek and follow only "Top-Dogs," and, so let it always be said that you never went back on what you heard from within. Only love and self-determination will bury the war hatchet, the war club, the hate, the evil cries, and if you are determined to make the world a better place because you have lived here, then peace will prevail. Remember always the lines from *The Ancient Mariner*: "HE PRAYETH BEST WHO LOVES BEST, ALL THINGS GREAT AND SMALL FOR THE DEAR GOD WHO LOVETH US, HE MADE AND LOVETH ALL."

Peace will always rule the day where reason rules the mind.

Let no one ever tell you what you cannot do. People who are afraid to try to conquer new lands, new horizons, will always tell you that it can't be done; but without any "quit-it" or "doubt-it," you tackle the thing that people say can't be done, and you will do it. The race is not to the swift, nor the battle to the strong, neither yet bread to the wise, nor yet riches to men of understanding, nor yet favor to men of skill; but time and chance happeneth to them all.—(*Ecclesiastes* 9:11.) If you never envy another man, you will find the place that God made only for you. When you envy another man, you miss the door of opportunity that closes for you. Envy is suicide, and hate is ignorance.

Thanks to all of you for your wonderful cards, your letters, your support, and most of all for your love and caring. We can all buy things, but to give of ourselves is truly the greatest gift of all. Always remember the promises we made here daily that you will continue to touch another child, and that child another child, and another. . .and yes, another, and then one day we will have just a little less darkness.

Go forward, children. Always go forward. The eyes of the world are upon you. The hopes and prayers of liberty-loving people everywhere march with you. Make the best of each day by hitting the line hard—don't foul, don't shirk, just hit the line hard. Remember it is better to die on your feet than to live on your knees beggin' and hoping! Go forward, always go forward. You MUST not fail. Go until the last energies are gone, go until the last hope is dimmed, and then go forth with the determination that this, too, shall pass away and tomorrow will be better because I worked so diligently today to make sure that there would be a tomorrow.

My thoughts are not your thoughts; neither your ways my ways, but take just a little sip of my determination, and when you have had your fill give heaping dosages to your children, to their children, and their children's children. The world will long remember what we do here, not what we say. Most of all, do not spend time trying to please people who cannot please themselves.

18.
Conclusions

Sophocles said: "Call no man happy until he has taken it to his grave." Therefore, it is difficult in my opinion to draw conclusions about life until it is over. However, at this point of my life, my conclusion is that "Life is like a football game-one cannot foul or shirk; we just have to hit the line hard."

Today's youth have grown up in an ambience of believing that we all live in a happy-ever-after world. They have also grown up in a very impersonal dial-a-friend, dial-a-prayer world, where people dial an 800 number for whatever ails them.

In the name of progress we have failed our children. Children today cannot tie shoelaces because they have velcro closures. They cannot tell time because digital buttons deprived them of this right. They do not learn the multiplication tables because we gave them calculators. The human voice reading a favorite bedtime story to children has been replaced by video cassettes. Family dinners have been replaced by the microwave oven and fast-food establishments. Even the fast-food chains have quality control, but we have seemingly lost control of the destiny of our children. In the name of relativity and easy choices, children today do not know which continent they live on and cannot name the five Great Lakes because we gave them more and more pictures in their textbooks and less text. In other words, we have been labeled educationally A Nation At Risk with 23 million illiterates and 35 million functional illiterates, and two million illiterates added to this dismal figure each year.

I therefore conclude at this moment of my life that the children who are being so dismally mis-educated today will one day lead us. What then? I further remind all freedom-loving Americans of the words of Thomas Jefferson: "Any nation that wants to be powerful and free and illiterate too, wants what never was and never shall be." I further conclude that all of us must once again relight the flickering candles of excellence in America. To ignore this plea is truly a sin of omission.

II.
Extraordinary Teachers

1.
My Living Philosophy as a Teacher

Jesus' disciples once argued loud and long as to which of them was the greatest. Jesus said, "He that givest most is the greatest. Living and teaching may be summed up on the language of the scripture: "Give and you will be given unto, search and you shall find. . .cast your bread upon the waters and it will return to you many fold."

As a teacher, I have found that teachers who give the most have the greatest return. Those teachers who cast their knowledge upon their students find that knowledge and more returned to them by their students. Supply your students with the best you have to offer and results will burst forth from students not as a product of their fetid past, but as an expanding product of a wonderful future.

Every individual has an urge to grow and become more than he is. Every child is born with the potential to become a lifter of the world, rather than a failing leaner. Every good teacher must insist that each student understand that it is his responsibility to make choices that will maximize productivity for both self and society; a person must be aware of the fact that he or she need not carry the emotional burdens of disadvantaged living throughout their lives. Supply each student with good thoughts and the opportunity to be all that he can be and convince him that straight thinking leads to better living. Once this realization is made, the student and his world will never resort to negative thinking again.

Show your students success once and they will never return to failure. Many of our students have never once in their lives known the light of success. Any average teacher can fail a student, but it takes an above average teacher to declare: "I will not let you fail." Average teachers are never in short supply and the good teacher will always make the poor student good, and the good student superior. A good teacher is always true to the Latin meaning of the word *teacher*, which means "to lead or draw out."

I believe that, like Pygmalion, I have the ability to sculpt my students into what I would like them to be. What a glorious and wonderful challenge! When I see the hesitant problem student who enters our school declaring to all "Teach me if you dare!" I think to myself, "Child, what joy awaits you." This student does not become a problem, but a challenge. My challenge is to show this child that his days of darkness, failure and lowered self-esteem are now over. It now becomes my chance to show this child that somewhere there is someone who cared enough to keep polishing until a shiny luster came shining through.

In my opinion, it is our responsibility as freedom-loving citizens to make the barren areas of our society fruitful again. It is our responsibility as good teachers to become discouraged with our students some of the time, but believe in their true worth all of the time.

The greatest enduring realities of life are still love, dedication, and service. These are the springboards that have allowed each of us to walk in the rays of freedom and liberty.

There are many problems confronting contemporary Americans, but if we have visited other countries we find that America is still the greatest country on earth. The preeminence we have known as Americans must be protected. We cannot be labeled *A Nation at Risk* and continue to go on as if all is well. We cannot afford to rest on our past laurels. Our past good will not save us.

The ability to change the world begins in the American classroom. If we allow our children to grow up believing that anarchy, crime, and destruction are a way of life, then we shall all be forced to suffer at the hands of our reluctance to act. The very children whom we miseducated in today's classrooms will one day lead us. If we have taught them that darkness and failure are a way of life, then we must realistically ask ourselves, "What are our chances of a prosperous future?"

I believe that it is impossible to put a Band-Aid on a hemorrhage. I therefore believe that, as well as learning to read, write, and compute, all Americans must learn the ethics, ideals, and the traditional values that made America a great nation in the first place. Any nation not imbued with these values is bound for extinction.

We must never forget the lessons of the ancient Romans. Rome was once considered the greatest society on earth. All roads once led to Rome. They, like us, however, began to think that their present greatness was eternal. We all know what happened to the Roman civilization. Educators must not ignore the symptoms displayed by their students. Our children's behavior tells us that enough is too much. Our children having children are loudly telling us that they seek love wherever and whenever they can find it. It may have proven to be counterfeit love, but we all need to be loved, wanted, and needed. Our children's abuse of drugs and alcohol is telling us that they need a balm to ease the hurt of never being able to find the elusive self-esteem and self-determination that we neglected to give them in our homes and classrooms.

I believe that each child who sits before a teacher is a champion worth wrestling. I believe that whatever we sow, we also reap. We have sown negative, insecure seeds, and the fruit we now reap is exactly what we have sown. We, as teachers and parents, must plant healthy trees so that the shade of the future becomes a bountiful refuge free of barren trees.

It is my job as a teacher to serve our children all the days of their lives, so that I may dare dream of a secure life for myself and the leaders of tomorrow that we teach today.

2.

Caring the Marva Collins Way

Often teachers develop belief systems about students and that is alright if those systems don't become rigid and inflexible, not allowing new evidence to come in and change them. Belief systems alter the way students are treated. If teachers believe that children cannot learn, those students, of course, will not learn. If teachers believe that the kind of home a student comes from has anything to do with what that child can achieve, then, of course, the curriculum becomes watered down and it becomes an impossible feat for the child to learn. I take the position that the more fetid a home environment might be, the harder a teacher must work to break that self-perpetuating cycle.

When I worked in Chicago's public schools, I often heard teachers say, "I am so sick of these children." When one takes this kind of attitude, it, of course, rubs off on the children. If we are not excited about what we do, then children can sense this. Can we imagine a doctor saying, "I do not believe this patient will ever get well?"

When we create a positive environment for our students, we can see some miraculous things happen. When we expose children to the great world masterpieces in literature, we always ask them, "Why are we reading this?" We let them know that great works are for great minds, and we do consider their minds great. When we use a vocabulary book for the younger children entitled, *Vocabulary For The College Bound Student*, we tell the students "YOU ARE COLLEGE BOUND." We give our students the idea that each of them is a winner. When children misbehave in school, we have "brainwashed" them to respond, when questioned about their behavior, that they are just too bright to misbehave. This, of course, cannot be just a one-day endeavor; it must be our consistent reply to them whenever problems arise.

Children respond to the "brainwashing" around them before they come to school; we at school must wash out the negative "brainwashing" and replace it with positive reinforcement. Just as the children have learned meanness, decadence, fetidness, and other negative attitudes, they must be re-taught by us the positive attitudes needed to win in life.

I care a great deal about our children, and they know this. How do we convey this attitude? Consistently, we tell our children that they are of royal blood, that they are born to win. We tell our children each day that they are special, unique, and this becomes a daily routine for our children. When we are constantly told that we are bright, we become bright. Of course, rhetoric is never a replacement for skills, and first we attempt to tell our children that they are bright, and then we use the positive attitudes that we have taught our children to encourage academic skills. We find that once we take care of the basic child, teaching then becomes an easier endeavor.

Thousands of visitors come to visit Westside Preparatory School each year to see what they call a miracle. We call it dedication, common-sense, determination, and a love for our students. We hope that the following information will help you see some of the miracles others come here to see, and hopefully your classroom too will become a beacon of hope for our children. . .the children who will one day lead us.

"Why aren't you going to continue talking to your friend?" Child responds, "Because I am too bright to waste my time."

"Turn around sweetheart, your life is in front of you; not behind you."

When a child calls another child a name or uses a racial slur then say, "Perhaps you would like to make an appointment with God and say, 'God you made something ugly and I am angry about that.'"

When a student passes a negative note written about the

teacher, say, "I love you too." Then continue teaching.

When a student insists on arguing a point, simply say in a soft and loving tone: "I love you very much and I will not let you fail."

When a student insists on talking more than he listens, say, "If God had meant for us to talk more than we listen, he would have given us two mouths and one ear; would you like to go and ask God for another mouth?"

Reinforce what has been learned in class. If a recently-introduced vocabulary word is appropriate, use it when speaking to a child. Say, for example, "I am *chagrined* at your behavior right now." Or we often use the lines learned from Browning's sonnet: "Let me count the ways I am going to punish you if you do not get in your seat." Or a children will write compositions as to why they are too bright to waste their time in school. We never use punitive lines to punish a child, such as: "I will not chew gum," etc. Instead, we have a child stand and give an impromptu speech about why he thinks he is too bright to waste his time in school; or we have him find the etymology of *gum* if he insists on chewing gum.

To get a rather rowdy and noisy group from the bathroom, say, "Out, out little spots, you should have taken care of that foolishness at home." (This, of course, is from Shakespeare's *Macbeth.*)

When a child makes a mistake, say, "If you cannot make a mistake, you cannot make anything." Create an ambience of positiveness in the classroom where children learn that it takes more courage to be wrong than to play it safe without ever responding to questions.

As simplistic as it may sound, love moves the world. Children respond to love and positive feedback rather than negative programming. Remember, you must be different— they have heard the negative comments all their lives.

Do not be afraid to be wrong and to admit that you are wrong. None of us have all of the answers all of the time. Have children proofread the blackboard for errors; remember, children cannot create havoc and find your errors, too. Make children a part of the learning environment.

Write encouraging notes to children, not just when they are in trouble. One troubled child got a note from me each day that said, "Charles was very, very, very, good today," and I signed it. He looked forward to taking this note home each day to a very negative parent. Soon, the parent too, became positive, and the parent looked forward to receiving this note each day. When the child did not behave, I would say, "What do you have to do to get your note today?" This was all I needed to curb this child's behavior.

Never resort to becoming child-like with your students. If a child persists in calling you names, consistently say, "I love you, and whatever you may call me or say, I still love you very much."

Some students are not easy to like, but never pick on a student. If you find a student with undesirable behavior, go out of your way to like this student, and you will find out that one day you will like the student.

Never place problem students in the corners or in the back of the classroom. Keep them near you; remember, we need to reach the troubled child quickly.

Touch students as you pass their desks and say, "Are you okay?"

Never let students say "I can't." Say to them, "We remove the 't' from the "can't" and we have "can."

Daily have the students repeat, "I am great, there is nothing that I cannot do. I am smart. I was born to win. I am royal. I am the greatest. . .I will not fail. This is a school where we learn to succeed. . .etc." Do this each day.

Write positive notes on the children's papers. When a child gets something wrong, do not red-mark the paper; take the child alone and help him get the errors right. Remember, if he had known how to do the paper correctly in the first place, he would have done it.

With child abuse being what it is today, avoid telling parents negative things about their children. You and the child attempt to solve the problems that arise in your classroom. You earn the respect and trust of your students, and you become a more effective teacher.

Stay out of the teachers' lounge, where you will hear negative things that will make you less of an effective teacher. Believe in your students; let no one break this trust. Do not send students to the office. Remember, you, the teacher, must be able to handle your own "family and your own household." Your household in this case being your classroom.

Do not become bound by the four walls of your classroom and the two covers of a book. Dare to bring in extra materials.

Never assign students what you have not read or do not know yourself.

Never teach so long that you feel that you have all the answers; you will never arrive in the Land of the Done.

Do not become a slave to teaching aids. You must become the master of your classroom. Do not assign reading groups. All children learn better when they are all taught together. Read orally, not silently.

Invite parents into the classroom, and not just when there is a problem. Have children write invitations to their parents that welcome them each day into the classroom. Do not talk to parents in academic vernacular which puts them out of touch with being able to communicate with you as a teacher. Be willing to bridge the gap with which your children come to you. Do not use statistics or the kind of home your children came from to determine what they can become. Remember, Abraham Lincoln did not learn to read until he was fourteen years old. What possible chance would he have in our classrooms today?

Positive Statements:

— You can make your life anything you want it to be.

— Every person has free will and can choose to make his life better or worse.

— School can give you the tools to lead a better life. We all come to make life better.

— The knowledge you put in your head is going to save you.

— You are so clever and so bright.

— You can do it.

— There are no excuses for not learning.

— Today will decide whether you succeed or fail tomorrow.

— We shall work together. I am always here to help you.

— I don't know everything, Children. I am learning all of the time myself. I am just another human being who's lived longer than you. I am not smarter. I am not greater than any of you.

— You can't be bright and stupid too.

— If you want to be a leader, you must learn to lead yourself first.

— You are what you learn.

— The world is not looking for average people.

— Where there is no order, there is disorder. Where there are ordered minds, there is an ordered society.

When a child is misbehaving say, "You knew how to do that when you came to school. Doing that (name the behavior) is a good way to get a job isn't it? Someone is actually going to pay you for doing that?"

When reading and students are not paying attention, say, "I am not here to entertain you. There is a lesson here. We had all better start paying attention to these lessons or this world is surely headed for trouble. I love you all the time even though I may correct you or disagree with you some of the time."

To a misbehaving child say, "That is not how the brightest child in the world behaves. You were born to win, so don't make yourself a loser."

To a child who is worried about lunch time or dismissal say, "Are you worried about getting one hour's worth of food when I'm trying to teach you how to get food for a lifetime?"

When a child gives an incorrect answer, say, "Very good try, but not quite."

When a child is not paying attention, say, "Pay attention.

Why? Because you are too bright not to."

Statement to develop trust: "I love you and I am not going to go home or to the teacher's lounge to talk about you behind your back. I am going to tell you the way it is to your face. Look at your (name a condition or a behavior: dirty face, torn shirt). Without a good education, you will always have that (name the condition). I expect you to act like someone who is getting an education starting right now."

Concentrate and you will radiate. Hold your head up high so that I can see your bright eyes.

Excellence is not an act but a habit. The more you do something the better you will become. Both statements can be used to inspire practice when practice becomes tedious.

Trust yourself. Think for yourself. Act yourself. Be yourself. Imitation is suicide. A statement reinforcing the importance of individuality.

Can you act like a bright child? If you know it then show it. If you can do it, then prove it.

State to the class that you have a room filled with mentally gifted minors.

ADD YOUR OWN IDEAS. . .

Ten Steps Toward Better Disciplined Classrooms

1. Always make friends with each student before there is a discipline problem.

2. Find something positive to say to each student everyday. Example: "My what nice gym shoes," or "I missed you yesterday, Cathy."

3. Give extra teaching time after school or before school to the slower student. This student is usually the one that causes havoc in the classroom.

4. Rather than eating with fellow teachers or staff, instead sit with a different child or the entire class each day.

5. When a student misbehaves, instruct the entire class that they are to repeat the following when asked why they will not misbehave. Your question: "Why aren't you going

to misbehave in class? Their response to you should be: "Because I am too bright to waste my time."

6. When younger students misbehave in class, do not have them write punitive lines: "I will not chew gum in class." Instead, have them write a composition on the etymology of *gum,* where gum came from, or a composition entitled *I Am Too Bright to Waste Time in School.* You may also choose to have them deliver a three-minute speech detailing *Why I Am Too Bright to Waste Time in School.*

7. Write positive notes on your students' papers, such as "Let's work on this paper *together*," or "I know that together *we* can do better."

8. Offer help to slower students with their schoolwork. It is usually these students who prevent teachers from accomplishing what they could with other students.

9. Never forget that you are a *professional.* Never resort to becoming a student. For example, when a student writes a note that says: "I hate you Mr. Jones." Read the note and say, "I like you too," and then call on that student to recite.

10. Reduce ridicule and laughter in the classroom by telling the student who speaks out that he or she is very courageous, and it took courage to be wrong, but they who stood silent or laughed took the easy path, and the child who speaks out is to be praised not mocked. Encourage students to clap for the other students; create a spirit of *group effort* in the classroom.

3.
A Tale of Two Classrooms

MRS. JONES: Good morning children. . .I am so glad to see you. I was so afraid you would not be here today. My! Robert, what a wonderful shirt, and just look at your lovely braids, Anna.

CHILDREN: Good morning Mrs. Jones.

MRS. BROWN: Hurry up and get in line! Shut up! Don't come in here with that noise. Robert, get in your seat now.

CHILD: Mrs. Brown, do you like my new gym shoes?

MRS. BROWN: Yes, yes, I see them; now sit down and be quiet.

MRS. JONES (to students who are a few minutes late): Good morning Cheryl, I am so glad you are here. I missed you yesterday.

CHERYL: I told my mother you would miss me Mrs. Jones, and I told her that I could not stay home today. My dress was dirty on the other side, but I turned it over so I could be here today.

MRS. BROWN: David, sit down right now. You come in here every day keeping noise and driving me crazy. I wish you would stay home. You are the worst child I have ever seen!

MRS. JONES: Robert, you are just too bright to keep that noise. Now you don't want to grow up to be a dummy do you? I knew you could do it. Good job. You are so bright! I am so proud of you!

MRS. BROWN: That's wrong. . .wrong. . .wrong. . .this is the sloppiest paper I have ever seen. You will never amount to anything. You will always be a dummy. [Child looks at sad face drawn on his paper; to fail at age 7 is quite traumatic.]

MRS. JONES: You wrote your name very neatly, Robert, but let's proofread this. [Note: teacher never said, "This is an error," but she uses the word, "proofread."] Don't worry about this, Robert; if we can't make a mistake, we can't do anything, and I have as much time as it takes to get it right, and besides, you learned something. . .you learned that this is not the way to do it. Let's give Robert a hand, class.

(The comments by both teachers are ones that I have actually heard used by teachers in the classroom. Which classroom would you like to be a part of? Mrs. Brown's or Mrs. Jones'?)

4.
Teaching Reading Comprehension to the Total Group

Before we assign questions at the end of a reading selection, each teacher should ask pointed questions during the oral reading.

Example: If you are reading *The Little Engine that Could,* ask the following questions as the child reads.

Question: What kind of hill did the little engine have to climb?
Answer: A steep hill, Mr./Mrs. _____ (*always have the children answer you in complete sentences*). Here, you are teaching adjectives as well as teaching reading.

She pulled and she pulled. She puffed and she puffed.

Question: What words show that the little engine was a hard worker?
Answer: She pulled and she pulled. She puffed and she puffed.

Pretty soon the little engine saw a big train, and she said, "Will you help me up the hill?"
The big train replied, "I have work to do. I cannot help you."

Question: What shows that in life we must help ourselves?
Answer: The child will reread the passage that answers
your question.

The little engine continued to say, "I think I can. . .I think
I can. . .I think I can. . .and then, I thought I could. . .I
thought I could. . .I thought I could. . .and finally she was
able to climb the steep hill.

Question: What shows that the little engine had determination? What does the word *determination* mean?
Answer: The child will reread the passage that answers
your question.

Ask each student, "What did you learn from this story?"
Discuss *attitude*. What does it mean? Have the children
discuss the axiom: "The attitude determines the altitude in
life."

After reading the entire selection, dictate the following
sentences to the students:

1. A little steam engine had a long train of cars to pull.
2. She pulled and she pulled. She puffed and she puffed.
3. "I think I can, I think I can," said the little engine.
4. The little steam engine sang merrily, "I thought I could,
I thought I could," and she did climb the steep hill.

(These sentences can be placed on the blackboard until
students are sophisticated enough to take dictation in their
seats.)

Question: What word in the first sentence tells us what we are talking about?
Answer: Engine.
Question: What is the subject of sentence number one?
Answer: Engine.
Question: What kind of engine?
Answer: Little, steam. Describe the engine.
Question: What word or words tells us what the engine did?
Answer: Had to pull.
Question: Had what to pull?
Answer: Cars.
Question: What kind of cars?
Answer: A long train of cars.

(This must be done for each story in order for children to understand. Consistency is the key.)

Now we will take this same story and use the following words for spelling words. Spelling words from the story *The Little Engine that Could.*

engine
indeed
sidetrack
alongside
scoured
merrily
finished
steam
slowly

Remember that when we assign an isolated spelling list, children learn to spell words just to pass a test and cannot spell the same words a week or so later. Teach spelling for a lifetime—not just to pass a test. We do this using the phonetic method.

Question: "Which *e* is in *steam?*"
Answer: *ea* says long *e* in *steam.*

In the word *merrily,* blank *y* says the sound of long *e,* and so does the *y* in the word *slowly.*

Also remember to syllabicate each word before assigning the list. Have each student repeat the words to be learned for spelling.

Rather than using isolated seat work, use the following for seat work.

1. A little _____ had a long train of cars to pull.
2. She came to a _____ hill. She _____ and she puffed.
3. The Little Engine said, "I _____ I can, I think I _____, I _____ I can," and she did get up the steep _____.

Have the class reenact the story. This increases their comprehension of the story. Have the children make invitations for another class and invite that class to their production. Teach them here the social meaning of *RSVP.*

Have one child become a reporter and interview the Little Engine. Create a newspaper headline regarding the Little Engine.

Teach alphabetical order by using spelling words from the previous page.

Have each child retell his favorite passage from the story, then have the child tell you why it is his or her favorite.

Do not teach in isolation. Whenever a child tells you that

he or she cannot do something, refer to *The Little Engine that Could*, until children learn to say, "I think I can, I think I can." After a child tries and succeeds, tell the child, "See, you thought you could and like the Little Engine, you did." Too often we teach in isolation. Remember to use the words from each story studied in daily conversation; otherwise we send a message to students that we learn words never to be used again.

5.
Developing Effective Reading Materials that Promote High Interest for All Students

Reading can be compared to the performance of a symphony orchestra. This analogy illustrates three points. First, like the performance of a symphony, reading is a holistic act. In other words, while reading can be analyzed into sub-skills such as discriminating letters and identifying words, performing the sub-skills one at a time does not constitute reading. Reading can be said to take place only when the parts are put together in a smooth, integrated performance. Second, success in reading comes from practice over long periods of time, like skill in playing musical instruments. Indeed, it is a lifelong endeavor. Third, as with a secure musical score, there may be more than one interpretation of a text. The interpretation depends upon the background of the reader, the purpose for reading, the amount of vocabulary the reader brings to the task, and the context in which reading occurs. [Taken from "What is Reading? The Report on Making a Nation of Readers," Department of Education.]

First we need to disband our traditional three reading groups—we need to teach beginning reading skills as a total group. For example: Phonics first before the whole-word approach. For example: we teach children the sound of "a"; why not teach them at the same time that the spellings are "a-e," "ay," "ea," "aigh," "eigh," "ay," and "ai." Why teach them some of the sounds and then later say, "These, too, boys and girls, are the sounds for 'a'." By teaching all sounds together, I have found that we prevent confusion of the spellings. The way we traditionally teach reading in American schools actually impedes the lifelong process of becoming a good reader.

When teaching the sound of "c," one should also teach that the these spellings make the same sound: "ck" as in "tack"; single "c" as in "cat"; "ch" as in "ache," "trachea," "bronchitis," "Achilles," "Andromache"; single "k" as in "king," "kill," "kilt," etc. This way the children will learn all the spellings for "c" at the same time. With daily dictation and patience, and yes, practice, the spellings become easy for the children. Also tell them the rule for the spellings of "ck" and that is: The vowel before "ck" is always short.

Before reading a Basal textbook selection, have the students pre-read the words to be read in the textbook by having each student take a turn, saying: "the word is *bat,* the vowel is *a,* as in *bat*"; "the vowel is *a* and the word is *bat*"; "the vowel is *o* and the word is *lot*"; "the vowel is *i* and the word is *hit,* " etc.

Develop a reading list and xerox or copy this list and set aside a time during the school day when each child individually reads the list by following the examples given above.

Each day the students should read as an entire group rather than following the traditional approach of three reading groups. Usually while the Red Birds are reading, the Blue Birds are causing discipline problems. When the entire group reads at the same time, this causes each child to pay attention, especially when the "Stop-Go" reading approach is used. It also helps with word recognition. For example, if one child calls a word "angle" instead of "angel," the other students hear the correction and they learn a new word. By having all students read orally, the teacher encourages comprehension and can immediately correct errors before they become permanent silent errors, never detected except on a standardized test, by which time it is usually too late.

When students read orally the teacher can ask for synonyms, antonyms or homonyms for words read rather than attempting to teach these in an isolated unit.

6

Allegory and Other Terms Explained

Abstract: Words that name quality or ideas such as kindness, forlorn, sagacious, etc.

Act: Division of a play.

Style: The way an author writes, his approach in his writings.

Allegory: Where characters and events are not real. Aesop is an allegorical writer. (People who write fables are allegorical writers.)

Alliteration: Same consonant sounds within a line. Example: "fillet of finny fish" is an alliteration.

Anecdote: A brief single incident within a writing.

Biography: The life of a person written by someone else.

Autobiography: The life of a person written by that person. If you wrote the story of your own life, that would be an autobiography.

Ballad: A poem that can be set to music.

Characterization: The technique used to show what a person is like. The characterization used in Marc Anthony's speech shows that he was very articulate, sagacious, peerless, and clever with words.

Assonance: Technique or methods used for producing a musical sound. For example, the bassoon in *Peter and the Wolf* represents the wolf.

Speaker: A person speaking (narrator).

Soliloquy: A speech spoken by one person. For example: Hamlet's query as to whether he should live or die.

Subjectivity: A personal attitude regarding a subject. To write from an opinionated point of view, to write from how you think or feel about a subject.

Suspense: Curiosity as to what will happen in a story. The high point of a story.

Satire: A serious situation made funny. George Orwell's *Animal Farm* is a satire of Russia. A person who writes satire is called a satirist.

Symbol: Something which represents something else. For example, the flag of the United States represents America; Batman and Robin represent good over evil; the rainbow represents rain, clouds, and thunder. Juliet, Pyramis, and Thisbe are symbols of love. Macbeth is a symbol of the struggle for power. Marc Anthony symbolizes how the right words can inflame people.

Tone: The expression of an author's attitude. Some authors use humor; some, such as Aesop, use a moralistic approach. Hans Christian Anderson illustrates his point by transforming ugly things into beautiful ones. The Greeks used the tone of courage, perseverance, determination, and hubris.

Word Choice: The words that an author uses. For example, Charles Dickens implies that a certain man's nose is long enough to be used as a hat rack. O. Henry describes Red Chief as a welterweight cinnamon bear.

Sonnet: A poem of fourteen lines. Petrach, Elizabeth Barrett Browning, and Shakespeare are some examples of sonnet writers.

Outline: A skeleton of an entire subject with main and subheadings.

Transition: The movement from one idea to another. The transition in *Hamlet* is from his deciding to kill himself to seeking revenge against his Uncle Claudius.

Rhythm: The beat of a poem.

Pun: A play on words employing the use of homonyms.

Scene: A division within the play.

Trilogy: A story that consists of three parts.

Haiku: A three-line Japanese poem with seventeen syllables.

7.
Teaching Shakespeare's *Macbeth*
(Grades 3, 4, and 5)

Locale of the Play: Scotland
Theme: Murder for personal gain.
Plot: Thou shall not kill.
Kind of Play: Tragedy. *Macbeth* is a tragedy because a tragedy gathers pathos and pity.

Suggested Activities:

Do background on William Shakespeare.

Do background on The Globe Theatre.

Point out Scotland on the map.

Teach children the British Isles by saying: England, Ireland, Scotland and Wales, four little puppy dogs without any tails.
Macbeth is the shortest of all of Shakespeare's tragedies.

The theme the seven deadly sins weaves its way through Macbeth. The seven deadly sins are: lust, hatred, envy, gluttony, slovenliness, pride, and sloth. Discuss how these sins apply to various characters in the play.

Puzzles of the play: pathos, hyperbole, symbolism, etymology, and tragedy.

Students should memorize the soliloquies from the play. Each student should be encouraged to read with tone. When this does not happen, the teacher should read for tone and delivery.

Double, double toil and trouble; fire burn and
Cauldron bubble.
Scale of dragon, tooth of wolf,
Witches' mummy, maw and gulf
Of the ravin'd salt-sea shark, root of hemlock
Digg'd i' th' dark,
Liver of blaspheming Jew,
Gall of goat, and slips of yew
Silver'd in the moons eclipse,
Nose of Turk and tartar's lips, finger of birth
Strangled babe ditch delivered by a drab,
Make the gruel thick and slab;
Add thereto a tiger's chaudron,
For th' ingredients of our cauldron.
Double, double toil and trouble; Fire burn and
Cauldron Bubble. Cool it with a baboon's blood,
Then the Charm is firm and good.
          (*Macbeth*, Act V:SC III)

"My eyes have made fools of all the other senses." What does this mean?

Lady Macbeth and Macbeth kill together, but they die apart. What does this mean?

The witches say, "You shall be King." However, they do not tell him the consequences. What does this mean? How does this apply to life?

The witches predict, but Macbeth must determine. What does this mean? How does society predict for us as a people?

The protagonist is the leading character in a play. Who is the protagonist in *Macbeth*?

Hyperbole is used extensively in *Macbeth* in the form of supernatural elements such as the ability to tell the future and poltergeists. What other supernatural elements exist in the play?

Shakespeare wrote *Macbeth* for King James, who was his cousin. Do you know the King James version of the Bible?

Can people make us evil, or is evil something that is inherent in all human beings?

Where does blame lie for Macbeth's situation? Is it with the witches, Macbeth, or both?

The antagonist of a play is one who competes with another in some way. Who is the antagonist of the play *Macbeth*?

What is even-handed justice?

What are naked frailties?

Write a character sketch of Macbeth and Lady Macbeth.

Discuss and define the following terms: devotion, patience, courage, fortitude, and ambition.

Why is there evil in the world?

"Time and hour runs through the roughest day." What does this quote mean?

What does "All the perfumes of Arabia cannot make these hands clean" mean?

What does the following statement mean: "She should

have died, hereafter. . .there would have been a time for such a word."

Who is Hecate? Does Hecate have a modern counterpart?

Describe Macbeth and Lady Macbeth.

Describe King Duncan.

What does the following statement mean: "What has made them drunk has made bold."

Who is referred to as a "Painted Devil"?

What does the following statement mean? "If chance will have me king, chance will crown me."

What does the following statement mean? "Why dress me in borrowed robes?" When someone calls you a name what are they dressing you in?

What is the insane root? Hemlock.

What does the "Milk of human kindness" mean?

What does "Vaunted ambition has overleapt itself" mean? What is vaunted ambition? Which character or characters display vaunted ambition?

"Out, damned spot! out, I say!—One: two: why, then 'tis time to do't—Hell is murky!—Fie, my lord, fie! a soldier and afeared?

"What need we fear who knows it, when none can call our power to account?—Yet who would have thought the old man to have had so much blood in him?" What does this mean?

What does the following mean? "The love that follows us is sometimes our trouble." How can love destroy us? Entertainers sometimes have fans that love them to death. What does this mean?

What does the following mean? "If it were done when 'tis done, then 'twere well it was done quickly."

What does the term "Bloody instruction" mean? Who gave bloody instructions? Who gives out bloody instructions today? What are those instructions?

What is drunk hope?

How does Lady Macbeth intimidate Macbeth into committing murder?

How do people try to intimidate you into doing something wrong?

What does the following mean? "It is a knell that summons Duncan to Heaven or to Hell."

What does the following mean? "Sleep no more. Macbeth does murder sleep; the innocent sleep that nourishes life." How does sleep nourish life?

What look likes an innocent flower, but is a serpent underneath? Do you know anyone like this?

"Confusion has made its masterpiece." What is the significance of this line?

Who can be wise, amazed, temperate and furious at the same time?

What does this mean? What is "The last syllable of recorded time?" Who speaks of this in the play?

"When our desire is gotten without content." What is the significance of this line?

What is doubtful joy?

"Things without remedy should be without regard." What does this mean?

What is the meaning of the following? "We have scorched the snake; not killed it." How is taking drugs analogous to "scorching a snake" and not killing it?

"I have stepped in blood too far to turn back now." Who made this statement and what does it mean?

What ingredients did the witches put into their foul brew?

What are some of the ingredients that witches of modern society put into their evil "brews"? How can one avoid these evil brews?

"Our fear makes us traitors." What does this mean?

"I cannot minister to a mind diseased." Who said this? Who is this person referring to?

"Pluck from memory a rooted sorrow." What does this mean? Who had a rooted sorrow?

"We are all players who strut and fret upon the stage and then is heard no more." What does this mean? How does this apply to life?

What is a tale told by an idiot full of sound and fury signifying nothing?

Have students reenact the play.

Have a trial for Lady Macbeth and Macbeth. Appoint a jury, attorney, judge, etc.

Have the children write their own version of the play.

Daily written compositions should be composed based on lines from the play.

Spelling words, dictation, and English lessons can also be taken from the play.

Define for children the term, "Blood will have blood."

Define the meaning of these words: "The sorrows upon the heart cannot be healed with medicine."

Discuss the etymology of words. Where do we get the word "Caesarian"? Julius Caesar was the first known person to be born by a Caesarian section.

8.
Teaching *Julius Caesar*

This lesson plan coincides with the original play *Julius Caesar* written by William Shakespeare. Grammar school children grades four and up can enjoy this play if it is presented in an informative and exciting manner. (No parts of this sheet may be reproduced or copied without permission.)

Words to Watch

Put these words on the blackboard before presenting the play. Never assign words for homework! These words should be looked up in the glossary or dictionary while the children are in class so that further synonyms, antonyms, and word study can be developed. All children should keep a reading folder. Words should be used consistently for spelling and dictation, also in the classroom for conversations. The purpose of learning is never pedantic; the child should be able to use what is learned forever.

1. Julius Caesar
2. Brutus
3. anachronism
4. blank verse
5. Globe Theater
6. William Shakespeare
7. England
8. Elizabethan stage
9. alchemy
10. aught

11. bestride
12. coronet
13. infirmity
14. intermit
15. lief
16. antagonist
17. protagonist
18. portentous
19. climax
20. lot
21. ummary
22. araphrase
23. oliloquy
24. rodigious
25. Casa
26. Cassius
27. Calpurnia
28. Triumvirate (rule by three)
    Ask, "Who are the triumvirates in this play?"

Characterization

CAESAR:
1. ambitious
2. reasonable
3. superstitious
4. infirm (He is deaf in one ear and has epilepsy.)
5. vain (He thinks only of himself and calls himself by his first name.)

CASSIUS:
1. envious
2. greedy
3. practical
4. scheming
5. a thinker

BRUTUS
1. integrity
2. unselfish
3. idealistic (He sees things the way he wants them to be, not as they really are.)
4. easily fooled
5. naive (He feels that everyone has good intentions).

ANTHONY
1. opportunist (He loves Caesar but seizes the opportunity to rule.)
2. articulate (He is a great orator; he has a way with words.)

SUPERNATURAL ELEMENTS IN THE PLAY
HYPERBOLE (HIGH-PER-BOH-LEE)
Caesar advises his wife Calpurnia to stand in the way of Anthony's whip so that she may bear a child. He listens to soothsayers (fortune tellers).

He consults the soothsayers and they advise him to beware of the Ides of March (March 15th). The wildness of the weather, the bloody dream of Calpurnia, and the bathing of the hands are also supernatural elements of the play.

Theme of the Play

This is a play which shows that the masses are fickle; they are always with whomever is leading at that particular time. Eventually the masses will always become unsatisfied with the leader they once lauded.

Point out to the children that they should watch for the development of each character. Examine the strengths and weaknesses of each character.

Julius Caesar is a tragedy. A tragedy shows the seriousness of a problem and has an unhappy ending.

Irony of the Play

If Caesar had heeded the dream of Calpurnia he would not have gone to the Roman Forum and ultimately to his death. Sometimes what we consider a weakness in us can be our own downfall.

Caesar's ghost appears to Brutus at Phillippi. We watch Anthony's metamorphosis into an ambitious man. Ironically, this is the reason that Caesar was allegedly murdered. Anthony becomes a ruthless member of the second Triumvirate. The children should note which three men rule throughout the play. This is called a power struggle. *Animal Farm* is analogous to Caesar because whoever rules makes slaves of the ruled. Anthony begins to want power for his own advantage. Remind the children of how Anthony changes throughout the play. In the beginning he truly loved and admired Caesar. Anthony offered Caesar the crown three times. What made Anthony change?

Brutus's weakness is his sense of honor and idealism. He again feels that everyone is honorable. Why is this a weakness?

Assorted Notes

1. Cassius, who is wise, could see that Anthony should not have had the opportunity to speak at Caesar's funeral, but Brutus ignores this warning.

2. The new Anthony emerges when he demonstrates his power to stir the people to act with words. The second Triumvirate emerges as Octavius Caesar (Caesar's nephew), Leppidus, and Anthony. Anthony develops a list of Romans who will be killed if they dare to oppose him.

3. In Caesar's case, power was not transferred to another man; it was ripped from him by his assassins. His death creates a struggle between Anthony and Octavius.

4. Caesar's power was actually used for the good of Rome: it brought new monies to Rome, he created public places for the citizens, he conquered new lands for Rome.

There is a Latin motto attributed to Caesar: "Vini, vidi, vici" which means "I came, I saw, I conquered." What does this have to do with Caesar?

5. Cassius kills because he is envious of Caesar's authority. He feels he is superior to Caesar. Brutus actually thinks he is acting for the good of Rome.

6. Caesar is a great man whose tragic fault is ambition. He felt that to obey supernatural signs was a weakness.

7. Anthony's soliloquy over Caesar's body reveals his desire to avenge his hero's murder. Caesar's ghost comes to avenge itself since Caesar sees that Anthony has changed.

8. A chance happening occurs when Pindarur comes; Brutus and Cassius both kill themselves because they feel that it is the enemy.

9. A character foil is when one character personally contrasts with another and therefore helps to explain the personality of the other character. Cassius and Anthony are both foils for Brutus. Cassius' personal greed, envy, and practicality contrast with Brutus's integrity, selflessness, and idealism. Anthony's shrewd political ruthlessness contrasts with Brutus' ingeniousness.

The Conflict of the Play

We see a conflict between a strong ruler and a group of men determined to kill him, they say, for the good of Rome. Each man has his own personal reasons, however.

Another conflict appears with the arrival of the second Triumvirate. There is a conflict between Brutus and Cassius; they are in conflict for the power of Rome. Brutus is suffering an internal conflict. It is between his allegiance to Caesar and his love for Rome.

He cannot decide which he loves more. This is analogous to Hamlet, who was also indecisive. How is Brutus indecisive?

Sample Worksheet for Julius Caesar

1. Why did Caesar want Anthony to hit Calpurnia with the whip?

2. The Ides of March is when?

3. Who said, "Let me have men about me who are fat; sleek-headed men and such as sleep o'nith. Yond Cassius has a lean and hungry look; such men are dangerous."

4. Explain: "lowliness is young ambition's ladder."

5. Who were the Tarquins?

6. Name the conspirators who killed Caesar.

7. Which assassin was the most sincere about killing Caesar?

8. Write Calpurnia's dream here.

9. What did the dream symbolize?

10. Who interpreted the dream the way they wanted it to be? What did this person say the dream meant?

11. Explain Artemidorus' speech here.

12. How constant does Caesar say he is? Explain.

13. Who is the first to stab Caesar?

14. Instead of saying: "Caesar is dead," what does Cinna say?

15. Which stab was the unkindest cut of all for Caesar and why?

16. How does Cassius try to convince himself that killing Caesar was a favor to Caesar?

17. Who does the servant say is wise, noble, and honest?

18. What does the word "lethe" mean?

19. Who is Ate?

20. Which man speaks to the crowd in an intellectual manner?

21. Which man appeals to the emotions of the crowd?

22. Which is strongest: Intellect or reason? Defend your answer.

23. Why is it good for people to often underestimate our abilities?

24. How many miles are in seven leagues?

25. Describe the character of Julius Caesar, Anthony,

Brutus, and Cassius here:

> Julius Caesar
> Anthony
> Brutus
> Cassius

26. What is the fatalism of the play?

27. Calpurnia says: "Your wisdom is consumed in your confidence." What does this mean?

28. What does Caesar mean when he says: "I have stretched in conquest mine arms too far to be afraid the tell the graybeards the truth?"

29. Who convinced Caesar to go to the Roman Forum?

30. Compare Caesar's line: "Nor heaven nor earth have been at peace tonight. Thrice has Calpurnia in her sleep cried out, help, ho, they murder Caesar" with the witches' lines from *Macbeth* that says "Macbeth shall sleep no more, Macbeth has murdered sleep, the innocent sleep that nourishes life."

9

Teaching Euripides' *Medea*

Before reading Euripides' *Medea,* I would suggest that the teacher read about Jason's search for the golden fleece to the children first. This will give the children needed background for the story. If materials are available, copy the story from a Greek Myth book and give all the children copies and have them read it as an entire class assignment before reading *Medea.* Suggested book: *Myths and Their Meanings* by Herzberg, published by Allyn and Bacon.

Prepare a fact sheet on Euripides from the encyclopedia. Remember, we want to make the children lifetime readers. This will encourage them to find more on Euripides and read more of his works on their own. Arrange several other of Euripides' works on a convenient table for children.

Write the following words on the blackboard before reading. Syllabicate each word. You, the teacher, enunciate each word, having the children repeat them after you. Then call on individual children to pronounce the words. Do this before reading *Medea.*

Words to put on the blackboard:

Ja-son

Me-de-a

Cre-on

Dra-ma (explain that the "a" at the end of the drama gets the German Schwa sound of "uh").

Eu-ri-pi-des (say to the children: Most Greek words are sounded out by pronouncing the second vowel as in Ae-sop, Aeschylus, etc.).

Cho-rus (explain that here the "ch" makes the sound of hard "k" and not "sh" as in Charlemagne, or "ch" as in "chair." Ask for other words with the hard "k" sound. Eg., ache, trachea, bronchitis, bronchial, chord, choral, etc. Explain how important the Greek chorus is in Greek drama. Tell the children what "drama" is.

Beginning the Lesson

Say to the children before the lesson: "Today, boys and girls, we are going to read a Greek drama by Euripides. This drama was written hundreds of years ago. However, it is as relevant today as it was when it was written. We will see that Euripides sympathized with the way women were treated long ago. He could actually have been said to be in sympathy with the present day's women's movement.

"Have you ever heard the aphorism that says: Hell has no fury like a woman scorned?' What do you think this means? Well, today we are going to read about how a woman gets revenge against her husband. We are also going to learn what happens when emotions take over reason. Which do you think is more important? Reason, emotions or intellect?"

After reading Euripides the children can use this for daily writing practice: Reason or Emotion? Be sure that each child understands reason and emotion.

Assign a group of children to read the chorus part. Assign different parts to each child so that each child is involved in the oral reading process.

Have the children read *Medea* orally to be sure that the children understand what they read. Ask questions as children read.

Additional Activities

Assign research on *Medea*.

Have the children write letters to Euripides, to Medea or Jason.

Pretend that you were Medea and you had to make up your mind to kill your children. What emotions do you think Medea felt before killing her children? Write these emotions.

Pretend that you were one of Medea's children. What would you have said when you found out that your mother was about to slay you?

What do you think happened to Jason after his children were murdered? Who is the antagonist in the story?

Who is the protagonist?

Dictate the following sentences to the children:

1. Medea felt that she had been scorned by Jason.
2. Jason felt great compunction at the murder of his children.
3. The children said, "Mother, do not kill us."
4. Medea said, "I will send gifts to the queen."
5. The chorus is used in many Greek tragedies.

Call the following words for spelling:
Medea
Jason
golden
fleece
Euripides
Greek
scorned
fury
Hell
emotion
reason
compunction

10

Teaching *The Song of Roland*

Time Scheme

Here is a list of events that occur in the story. In the blanks at the left, number these events in relation to the order in which they happen in the story. Note: Certain events or statements or positions are repeated throughout the story for emphasis. Mark these events in the order in which they occur.

_____A. Roland defends his mother when Charlemagne sends his retinues for Roland and his mother.

_____B. Roland has flashing proud eyes.

_____C. Roland becomes a knight in the court of Charlemagne.

_____D. Roland takes wine and goodies from the king's table.

_____E. The king is having a feast.

_____F. Roland said, "These arms are my mother's cup-bearer."

Dictation to be Given From the Story

Use the blackboard and read each sentence aloud once, then dictate the sentences. After repeating the sentence aloud in unison, the students should write it on alternate lines of ruled paper. One child goes to the blackboard to write the sentences, those students at their seats copy the sentences. This is a whole class approach.

Subject Pronouns

The word a noun or pronoun refers back to is called an antecedent. Have the children pick out nouns, pronouns, and other parts of speech from the following sentences.

1. In this story the king and his knights are having a feast.
2. He takes the choicest food to his mother.
3. She questions him.
4. The squire said, "You and the beggar woman must follow us."
5. Roland defends her.

Example: Which five words are the subject of sentence one? Which five words tell us which people are having a feast? (The king and his knights).

Epics

This story is an excerpt from *The Legend of Roland*. All epics begin *in medias res*. This is Latin for "In the middle of things." When all epics begin, the action has already begun. Example: In the epic *Paradise Lost*, by John Milton, the Devil has already taken over Heaven. The Spanish epic is titled *El Cid*. The French Epic is called *The Song of Roland*, or *Chanson De Roland*. The German epic is *The Story of Siegfried and the Dragon*, or *The Niebelungenlied*. All epics are stories of heroic deed. The English epic is *Beowulf*. *The Divine Comedy* by Dante Alighieri is an Italian epic. Other epics include *Song of Hiawatha* by Henry Wadsworth Longfellow (1855), *John Brown's Body* by Stephen Vincent Benet (1928), *Conquistador* by Archibald Macleish (1932), and *Paterson* by William Carlos Williams (1946).
Background of The Song of Roland

The origin of this eighth-century French epic is obscure, but the story is based on a battle between the Gascons of Spain and Charlemagne of France.

This epic glorifies Christianity, but among the early Christians of Western Europe it was generally believed that "pagans" should either be converted or killed. In this epic, *The Song of Roland*, Christianity provides moral justification for Charlemagne's campaign, but in actuality, his motives were not entirely religious.

Courage, valor and honor are the most cherished values in *The Song of Roland*. Ganelon, Roland's step-father, lacks all three and is suitably punished. Roland's suffering is rooted in his unrelenting pride. Even when surrounded and outnumbered by a horde of enemies, he hesitates until the last possible moment before summoning Charlemagne's help, feeling it is more noble to fight valiantly against all odds. Only when Roland is defeated does he blow his ivory horn for help.

> *Count Roland's mouth with running blood is red;*
> *He's burst a sunder the temples of his head;*
> *He sounds his ivory horn of anguish and distress.*
> *King Carlon hears, and so do all French.*
> *Then said the King, "This horn is long of breath."*
> *"Tis blown," quoth Naimon, with all a brave*
> *man's strength.*

Write similes from the story.
Write the adverbs from the story.
Write ten nouns from the story.

Who Are We?

I am an unusual guest, I am bold, I am self-confident. Who am I?
I am King of the Holy Roman Empire. Who am I?
I am Bertha. Whose mother am I?
I am Charlemagne's father.
I am a small town about 30 miles north of Rome.

Composition

Write a one-page composition entitled *The Qualities of Leadership*. Relate how Roland displays these qualities.

Discuss the traits of a leader (perseverance, determination, stick-to-it-iveness and self-esteem) before writing compositions. Mediate errors as the children write before they become remedial errors.

True or False

1. _____ Roland was very brave.
2. _____ Roland was Charlemagne's son.
3. _____ *The Song of Roland* is an epic.
4. _____ The word "chivalry" deals with the rules and customs of medieval knighthood.
5. _____ "Palfrey" refers to a riding saddle horse, especially a gentle one.
6. _____ Charlemagne was King of the Franks and The Holy Roman Empire.
7. _____ "Insolence" means "nice, kind, or gentle."
8. _____ Epics begin *in medias res*.

News Article

You are a news reporter. Interview Roland after he leaves the banquet hall.

Dramatic Structure

Exposition
Sets the scene, gives necessary information about the circumstances in the story.

Statement of Theme
A character's speech that summarizes the writer's message.

Character Development
Information about a character's past that helps the reader understand a character's many facets.

Background
Summarizes events of the past that have a bearing on present action.

Conflict
Battle between two people, two factions or two ways of thinking.

Predicament
Facts about a character's circumstances that makes the conflict more urgent.

Change in Circumstance
A twist in the plot that increases the character's predicament.

Crisis
An event that brings the conflict to a head.

Resolution
Releases the tensions of the conflict, creates new circumstances so that the character or characters can carry on their lives, or a situation that changes the character's lives for better or worse.

Details
Each of the phrases below describes one of the characters in the story, *The Song of Roland*. Write (R) if the statement applies to Roland. Write (C) if the statement applies to Charlemagne. Write (B) if the statement applies to Bertha. Write (D) if the statement applies to the Dwarf. Write (S) if the statement applies to the Squire. Write (N) if the statement applies to Naimon. Write (M) if the statement applies to Malagis.

"I welcome firmly since I recognize you as my brother."

"Ha, my brave me!" He cried in tones of merriment. "What have we here? Twelve gallant squires in combat with a single boy."

He told Bertha of Roland's strange daring deed in the feast hall at Sutri castle.

"Mother, I have brought you your share of the feast."

Then he placed before her the bread and the wine, a delicately baked fowl, and rare fruits, and while she ate, he told her of what had happened to him.

"What say you, sir wizard?"

She sat in the lonely hermit cell awaiting the return of her son.

"Indeed, that is a bold boy. He will make a brave knight."

"The slave gathers nuts in the forest. To my mother belong the very best things that your table affords."

"The choicest game, the rarest fish, the reddest wines are hers."

"He has a proud step and flashing eyes."

He was as fearless as a young eagle. He gazed into the face of the king.

Comprehension
It was a great day in _____.

Indeed, said Charlemagne, "That is _____. He will make a brave knight."

"The line drinks from the brook," answered _____ proudly.

Your mother must be a _____ lady.

And who is her cup _____? Come tell me about it.

The chamber halls were filled with knights and _____.

I doubt if ever more _____ was seen in the castle hall.

Mirth and _____ ruled the hour.

"Stop!" cried the King. "How dare you be so _____."

He seized upon a _____ of rare line and a loaf of line that had been placed before the king.

"My Lord, the lad is no _____."

"Mother, I have brought you some share of the _____."

Were they knights, or even _____, I would go with them; but they are neither.

And then Naimon told her of Roland's strange, _____ deed in the line hall at the line castle.

In spite of himself, a _____ smile played upon his face, and his eyes line merrily.

Points of View
Mirth and revelry ruled everywhere.

_____

_____

_____

_____

Those who stood around were awed by the lad's proud bearing.

_____
_____
_____
_____

"The peasant drinks from the brook," answered Roland proudly.

_____
_____
_____
_____

Roland, without a word dropped the club to the ground, and promised to go with the good knight at once if he would only find some means by which his mother might be helped to reach Surti castle without the fatigue of walking.

_____
_____
_____
_____

Analogies

_____ is to fearless as trainers are to lions.
_____ is to fruit as painting is to original.
_____ is to knight as combat is to soldier.
_____ is to boy as bravery is to knight.
_____ is to revelry as fun is to conviviality.
_____ is to rare as food is to delicacy.

Antonyms and Synonyms

Write an antonym, synonym, or homonym for each word:

dire_____

hypocrite_____

courage_____

ere_____

dais_____

sage_____

Character Sketch of Roland

_____
_____
_____
_____

11.
Why I Teach

Often I am in the company of people who run billion-dol-lar corporations and have amassed fortunes through the expertise of selling one product or one service or another. These people seem to have all of the material things that are inherent in our idea of the American Dream. It is during these moments that I reflect again and again as to why I teach.

When I return to the classroom and see children's eyes holding wonder like a cup, then I know why I teach. I hear a child say, "I love you, Mrs. Collins," and I am the recipient of many gifts such as rings that tarnish or candy that is sticky from being in a sweaty palm (and I must courageously eat that piece of candy given to me by a benevolent child); or a child says to me, "You smell good; I love you.". . .I then know why I teach.

When I see a precis written by my students filled with ideas germinated in my classroom, and when I hear ideas that I have given expanded upon with lofty thoughts of their own, I know why I teach.

I then, too, think that most human beings are as good as they are because some unknown teacher cared enough to continue polishing until a shiny luster came shining through; because some teacher cared enough to remove the previous fetid tags and labels of failure from their psyches.

I then think of how many times visitors from all over the world have come to Westside Preparatory School and replied: "It's amazing what you do here with children." I then think how many times we have called the profits of a billion-dollar corporation a miracle; we expect profits; we expect success. Why then can't we expect the same success from our children? That is why I teach.

Then there is Tiffany, a child considered autistic and who had not spoken, who had been told by the experts that she was an unlovable and unteachable child. Then one day after much patience, prayers, love, and determination, Tiffany's first words to me were "I love you, Mrs. Ollins." The consonant "C" was left off; but I realized that the tears that flowed from Tiffany's declaration made me the wealthiest woman in the world. Today, to see Tiffany writing her numerals, beginning to read single words, talking, and most of all to see that glee in her eyes that says, I too, am special, I too, can learn—this is to me worth all of the gold in Fort Knox.

I don't know much about tax-shelters, balance sheets, and takeovers mentioned in big business, but the biggest business on earth to me is to see a child whose eyes proclaim you his or her heroine.

Another reason I teach is Durvile. Durvile is a student from the Cabrini-Green Housing Project. This is an area where one keeps score of the murders, rapes, and crimes that prevail in the area every minute. Yet, this lad came to our school in September with a fourth-grade level in reading and now in April he has scored at a twelfth-grade reading level. Durvile squints, because he has difficulty seeing, yet despite the odds, he is the brightest lad we have ever had at our school. Durvile confuses the statisticians and the people who do all of the baleful studies as to what one can become when one is a resident of a fetid area. Right on, Durvile— one day you will show the world that all you need is an opportunity. Despite the fact that you are not a paying pupil at Westside Preparatory School, and we are always financially strapped, it is worth all of my sleepless nights wondering how I am going to balance our deficits to see the glow in your eyes that will one day light the world.

There is Takiesha, a three-year-old who is reading, knows her alphabet, and can compute with two-digit numerals and takes pride in her knowledge, proving again that young children can do more than take naps, drink milk, and go home at the end of an average school day.

These are the real reasons I teach. To see people grow right in front of my eyes is truly God's work on Earth; it is my miracle. It is the kind of miracle that one cannot see from totals on a balance sheet, from profits and take-overs. I may not be mentioned in *Forbes* magazine as one of the wealthiest women in America, but my wealth cannot be measured on a balance sheet. I do not have financial power, but I have the power to mold, to nurture, to hold, to hug, to love, to cajole, to praise, and yet criticize too, to point out pathways. . .to become part of another person's well-being. What could be more powerful?

Repeatedly I have seen myself intoxicated with the power of taking child after child written off in other systems and with constant nurturing blossom into seeds of fruition here. . .I now do not believe that any child cannot be taught something.

Being a teacher is to become a part of a kind of creation. A creation of knowing that miracles occur because you cared, loved, and patiently kept polishing until the dark corners of a child's mind become brightened, and as you watch those formerly sad eyes become luminous, you then know why I teach. You know that there is no brighter light ever to shine than that which comes from a child's eyes formerly hidden in the dark.

Then there is Kevin Ross. Kevin was a twenty-four-year-old college athlete who had spent four years at Creighton University and came to Westside Preparatory School reading at a second-grade level. I watched Kevin's ambivalence fade away as he learned the printed word, he learned grammar, and he learned that the light of literacy could be his domain. Today, as he speaks at such places as Harvard University and can hold his own on shows such as "Face the Nation," I know too, that teaching is the greatest profession on earth.

I teach because I believe Plato was right when he said, "Education is cumulative and it affects the breed." To think that I have given a generation the torch of literacy that can be passed to their heirs is truly the denouement of living. To think that I have been a small part of a miraculous living person is truly God's work here on Earth. To know that though much has been taken from most of the students who enroll at Westside Preparatory School, I believe that much still abides and I am willing to work as long as it takes until each student finds their rightful potential.

I teach because I am there when the first breath of knowledge comes shining through and I too can then catch that breath of fulfillment that comes from knowing that I was a small part of that breath of revitalization.

I teach because I do not have to worry about children thinking that I want something in return when I hug them, when I say, "I love you and right now I need a big hug." I do not have to worry that I will be called a phony because I care. Children are like the Velveteen Rabbit we read about in the classic story of what it's like to become real. Children are real and they can never become unreal once they find someone who really, really loves them for what they are with a genuine respect for what they can become. That is why being real does not happen to adults, because they do not understand. Adults are too easily hurt, and they have to be carefully kept, and therefore, the real world is an illusive one for them. This is the reason I teach.

I teach because a withered orange given to me by a child is a gift of love, and not a bribe for my favor. A happy face drawn on a child's paper is his paycheck, and it draws a smile more quickly than all of the toys that parents buy at Christmas time.

I found that teaching offers more than money. It offers love. It offers something that most people spend a lifetime unable to obtain.

I teach because of Sam, the young man put out of another school for throwing an eraser. After just four months at our school he has won a National Merit honor and scored so high at his selected high school for September that he has been given a scholarship. I teach for Sam, who will one day make a real contribution to America and the world; to know that I have been a small part of that contribution is to me the greatest power on earth.

I teach because, after being told day-by-day that I am loved, I begin to love myself more, and I find that I have even more love to give. And that is why I teach.

The Principles of Good Teaching

FAITH
Just as faith moves mountains, faith in your students moves them to heights never imagined.

HARVESTING
Make this day the greatest student harvest ever because you refused to let your students fail.

FAITHFULNESS
Insist on faithfulness over the little things. E.g., insist on elan in the way a child enters the door, keeps his or her desk, heads his or her papers. Getting the little things right makes the bigger things easier also.

DON'T BE A JUDAS
Never betray your students' confidence. Become their teacher some of the time, become their friend all of the time. Never write negative comments on their records. Today's problem student could become tomorrow's leader, and all because you cared enough to polish that child's mind until the luster came shining through.

TEACH EVEN THE LEAST OF THEM
Stop ink-blotting, testing, and measuring until there is nothing left but lowered self-esteems. Teach as if every child, regardless of background, ethnicity, or socio-economic background were a son or daughter of Harvard or Yale graduates.

TEACH BECAUSE YOU CAN'T HELP IT, NOT FOR WHAT YOU ARE PAID

Teach with a passion. Teach with a steel trap determination that says, "I will not let you fail."

GO INTO THE SCHOOLS AND SPREAD YOUR GOSPEL

Teach so deliberately that even the most recalcitrant student drops his or her weapon of indifference and lack of motivation.

TEACH AS IF YOUR VERY LIFE DEPENDED UPON IT

Attitudes are catching. Children are extensions of us. When we make lessons come alive with what I like to call *Hot Teaching*, every child becomes a winner.

I COME AS A TEACHER TO SAVE YOU, NOT FAIL YOU

Any average teacher can fail a student. Superior teachers who never anchor themselves in mediocrity will always make the poor student good, and the good student superior.

DARE TO BE DIFFERENT

When others declare a child a failure, dare to say, "I will be the one to save you, child." If at first you don't succeed, keep trying, knowing that just one more time will let you declare a *fait accompli!*

III.
Inspiration For Us All

1.
I Celebrate Me

Despite all the negative cries and predictions about what I am. . .what I will become. . .and the fetidness of my environment. . .I will never hide my humiliation by pretending to be tough and callous and establishing a destructive attitude. I will let others predict, knowing that only God and I can determine my fate. I celebrate me. I celebrate me because I am special, I am unique, and there is no other like me. Because I am eager to defy the odds of statistics, I will spend my lifetime conquering cold statistics and achieving success. I celebrate me. My record may not say much about me personally, but numbers rarely reflect anyone completely. All I ask is an opportunity to become a lifter rather than a leaner in society. All I ask is a chance to march in the manly mainstream of society rather than becoming a passive bystander catching the crumbs of others. I celebrate me.

I will ingeniously ignore the free-to-fail tickets that society offers me. I will avoid failure in all of its vilest forms because I celebrate me. I celebrate me because I refuse to go through life attempting to become a live wire that will eventually become a downed power line spewing hate and destruction. I celebrate me. I celebrate me by making my every effort a superior effort. I celebrate me because I know that life is calling me, and that there will be worlds unfolding unto me. The dreams of success beats loudly in my saddened chest, but I still celebrate me. I celebrate me despite the blurred visions, the dimmed aspirations, the deprived enigmas, the poor teachings, the broken quests, and unfinished dreams, the never-ending shadows, the carpets of glass instead of carpets of grass, the inadequate compassion, the unannounced failure notices, the unanswered yearnings, and the endless journeys. . .I still celebrate me.

I celebrate me because it is impossible for society to look into the seeds of time and determine which seed will grow and which will not grow. I celebrate me because failure has woven a masterpiece of those who did not celebrate themselves. I celebrate me so that nothing will ever prevent me from celebrating others.

2.
Every Inch a Teacher

"As the blinded and spurned Duke of Gloucester encounters the ragged and spurned King Lear, he still says that he is every inch a king."
—From *King Lear* by William Shakespeare.

The unattractive child, the child from a poor home. The statistically written-off child, the statistically inferior child, the child from a single-parent home—all of these children can become tall candles if you are willing to be the wick that lights them. If we can only be Every Inch a Teacher at all times and realize that each child is a champion worth wrestling.

Here sits Johnny, declared learning disabled, but you, the Every Inch a Teacher, declare him only the victim of some teacher's inability. You will become the Pygmalion who will sculpt, carve, and mold until that child becomes what the naysayers say he cannot be. You will bring the light to that child's life. You will be the one that discovers light in that child's eyes that makes Fort Knox lackluster by comparison. You are Every Inch a Teacher. You are the teacher Socrates was. You are the teacher who taught blind Helen Keller. Remember Annie Sullivan who saw not Helen's blindness, but her true potential. Remember that the teachers who taught Abe Lincoln never reminded him that a nonreader at age 14 was an impossible student. Remember Alexander the Great, who spoke the following of his teacher, Aristotle: "My parents gave me life, but Aristotle taught me how to live it." Think of David Copperfield, who speaks the following of his teacher Agnes: "May you never leave me except to better yourself, and may bettering your-self render itself impossible so that the shadows I now dismiss still find you among me pointing upwards." Teachers who are Every Inch a Teacher are always among their students, pointing upwards. Bettering themselves is an impossible feat because they do every day what they love with a passion that they never lose. Because they are Every Inch a Teacher, they remain forever among their students, always pointing upwards.

Teachers who are Every Inch a Teacher take the spurned, the ragged, the disenfranchised seeking literacy and they give those huddled masses the freedom that all literate people seek.

3.
Foolish Inconsistencies

Ralph Waldo Emerson said, "A foolish consistency is the hobgoblin of little minds." Far too many educators continue the foolish consistency of a "bad" script given them by their teachers, and they devote lifetimes to passing this script on to their students; their students pass it on to their children, and to their students. . .and therefore the foolishness never ends.

Children respect teachers who at all times show that they are concerned about their students. Children easily detect false voices, eyes that never meet theirs, hurried answers, impatient retorts. In other words, children are great barometers of what we actually are. It is easy to fool adults; but children know—they can read our souls, our hearts, and the veneer of facetiousness is never thick enough to hide the real us from children.

Many of us can be excellent for a day, but we find a lifetime of excellence to be just a bit difficult. Good teachers leave their egos and problems at the door each morning. They become so immersed in the children they teach that they forget time, problems, who they are, or what they can't do. They believe that they exist for their students. They hear with their hearts, they see with their souls, and they teach with their conscience. The good teachers realize that some- one watered their dreams, and it becomes their lifetime quest to water new dreams. They become living examples of compassion, they become the answers to failure, they are the gifts of empathy, and they leave every classroom every day, every moment, every second, with the knowledge that the light that shines in their students' eyes is a light that they inspired. They believe that all children's eyes can truly hold wonder like a cup.

4.
Screw Your Determination to the Sticking Place and Our Students Will Not Fail

As Macbeth decides whether to slay King Duncan or not to slay King Duncan, Shakespeare has him say to Lady Macbeth, "What if we should fail?" She replies, "We fail?. . . We will not fail, screw your courage to the sticking place. . ."

Let us as teachers and parents screw our courage to the sticking place and our children will not fail. When our children make mistakes, let us use great classical books to teach them lessons that they never could have mastered had it not been for the mistake. Let us make national headlines that say, "American students top other nations academically." Those of us with just an iota of American spirit left can do it. Great American teachers across our fruited plains, our snow-capped Rockies, and our wheated fields can do it. We are a "Can-Do" nation. We are a preeminent nation. We are a nation of believers of the American dream. We will not tolerate the American nightmare outdistancing the American dream. We will become vaulting ambition that will leap over decadent failure. We will become the Pygmalions of our time, determined to carve our own destinies through the children who will one day lead us.

We will fire the imaginations of our students. We will leash the last remnants of failure. We will remain true to our credo that we were promised the pursuit of happiness, and, therefore, we will give our children the skills to pursue that happiness and self-esteem. If together we screw our determination to the sticking place, our children will not fail.

5.
What a Piece of Work is a Child

"Noble in reason, infinite in faculties, in form and moving.
How express and admirable. . .In action, how like an angel. . .
In apprehension, how like a god! The beauty of the world. . .the paragon of animals."
—From *Hamlet* by William Shakespeare

Shakespeare declares, in the play *Hamlet,* "What a piece of work is a man." I declare, "What a piece of work is a child." Think for a moment—here is a fresh, new piece of clay that we as teachers have the ability to make our indelible mark on. We must carve well, for once that child comes to us as an adult, we have either carved well, or we can carve no more. What a glorious opportunity! A child is noble in reason, in faculties, and in form and moving, how express and admirable. In action, how like an angel. . .in apprehension, how like a god! The beauty of the world, the paragon of animals. And so states Shakespeare in *Hamlet.* But what a wonderful legacy for a teacher!

The child comes to us trusting, naive, pure, uncarved. . .a piece of sponge ready to soak up all the knowledge we are willing to give. What excitement this child generates! He or she is ours. We are his captors. We are his gods and goddesses. He hangs on our every word. His eyes are ours. We can either make those eyes hold wonder like a cup, or. . .yes, we can make them as dead as lead. A child is the pencil that comes to us without knowledge of what to write on the paper of life. Let us be that piece of paper that shows the "pencil" what to write. . .how to write. . .and how to write a legacy that will make America the great country it can be and it was meant to be. Let us make this masterpiece. . .the child. . .a work of art for the world to admire.

A child is noble in reason, infinite in faculties, and his movements are admirable. If he realizes that you love him, he is like an angel. He is indeed the beauty of the world until, somewhere, someone teaches him to fail, to be mean, to distrust, to become a demon. Inside each child is an angel just dying to get out. When he finds that very right teacher who gives him the key to unlock the demons and let the angel come forth, he becomes our victim for life.

A child is forgiving, loving, and ready for sculpting. He can be anything we'd like him to be; meanwhile, he can be nothing if we choose. We are his captors. We are his future. . .we are his lifeline to the real world.

A child carries a written signature of the author of their lives. Is your signature written there for better or for worse? Does this child bear your stamp of approval? Have you validated this child to go forth winged by your heart desires, to find the riches unknown in self-esteem, self-determination? Have you yet discovered the miracles of a child? Have you yet heard those wonderful words, "I love you so much"?

6

The Greatest Love of All

(Written for My Students,
March 7, 1981)

Don't spend so much time trying to wriggle down inside of my skin trying to tell me what I can or cannot do; I can do anything if you, Teacher, do not teach me too thoroughly that I can't.

Don't let me get away with everything I try to get away with; I am only testing you, Teacher. It makes me feel secure when you let me know that I have limits. I only want to see how much I can get away with. Be willing to polish, Teacher, until my real fervent luster comes shining through.

Don't try to make me feel smaller than I am: I realize that you are bigger than I. When you try to make me feel small, it only makes me try to be "big."

Don't get upset at everything I say; it is only my way of saying, "I, too, want to be accepted by you, and ultimately by the world." Please teach me, Teacher; clowning gets to be too much of a chore. It is easier to perform in what I know I can do best—being a lifter of this world; being a leaner is just too hard.

Don't tell my parents everything I do, Teacher. Can't we work out our problems between the two of us? Make today worthwhile so that I may dare to dream of a tomorrow. Remember I only live for today. Your opinion of the future is much greater than mine.

Don't nag. If you do, I shall have to protect myself by being smart enough or sassy enough to protect my image with my peers. Praise me, Teacher, for what I do get right; remember, it takes courage to be wrong. Didn't you ever make mistakes, Teacher? Tell me, Teacher, that if I can't make a mistake, I can't make anything.

Don't get upset when I say "I hate you." It is only because I can find nothing better to say with all of the bad thoughts coming with such rapidity within. Teach me better ways to express my anger and frustrations. Teach me to use my time wisely. Remember, I know nothing of the value of time.

Don't make the school day so boring, Teacher. Can't you compete with the television set? If you can do this, Teacher, then there will be no reason for me to turn the television set on.

Don't tell me that my fears are silly; they are very real to me. Be patient when you do my report card, Teacher. How would you like to go home with a report card to be ridiculed by your family? Help me to get things "right" before I get them "written."

Don't tell me to call you if I need help, Teacher; I don't always know when I need help.

Don't brag about your being perfect, Teacher; it confuses me when you too make mistakes.

Don't always ask the smartest children to help you with the chores; I would like to be useful, too, Teacher. When you don't ask me to help, I then find ways to aggravate you. It is the only way I can get the bad feelings out of me.

Don't be afraid to say that you made a mistake, Teacher. To be human is to make mistakes.

Don't forget how quickly I am growing up, Teacher. I must go through my different stages of development. Don't expect me to have all of the answers all of the time. Please do not try to mold me into what you'd like for me to be. Please let me be what God intended me to be; remember, a plant cannot be a weed.

Don't write me off so early, Teacher; I am still learning and developing. Teach me, Teacher, as if you were proud of my efforts. When you are so critical, I simply stop trying.

Don't teach me because it is your duty; show me that I am an individual and that you care. Say something to me besides what is in your line of duty. Can't you notice my new gym shoes or my new shirt? Tell my parents something good about me. Please don't always tell them all of the things that I do wrong—don't I do anything right? I cannot survive without lots of love, patience, understanding, and I need your help. Please do not tell me to sit down and shut up. Make me know that my questions are never silly and that the more I can ask you, the more I will learn. Treat me fairly, the way you treat your friends—then I will learn to trust you.

I learn more from what you do, Teacher, than I do from what you say. Please do not expect me to do my homework when you leave each day with your books neatly stacked on the desk. If you are enthusiastic about teaching, that enthusiasm will rub off on me.

Don't tell me that you don't care whether I learn or not; I will never try again. Please help me to get a paper hung on the walls, too, Teacher. I pretend not to care, but it really hurts to see the same children get praised all of the time.

When I am a new student in your room, Teacher, don't tell me starchily to take a seat. Please introduce me to the children in the room and please assign me a friend until I can find my way. Adjusting to a new school and new friends can be very painful.

Don't give me homework to do and tell me to figure it out for myself. If I had the answers, Teacher, I would gladly put them there to get your praise.

Don't give me a fish for a day, Teacher; teach me to fish forever.

Don't act as if you expect nothing from me, Teacher; I then have nothing to live up to.

I love you Teacher; I want your acceptance. I act up only because I, too, want you to pay me some attention before I get into trouble. Touch me, Teacher, before I am in trouble, and I will know that you care all of the time and that you are only aggravated with me some of the time.

Rather than yelling, say to me, Teacher: "I love you, but I will not let you fail. Get in your seat so that you can have choices in this world." Write me a special note on my paper, Teacher. I get so tired of seeing all of the things that I do wrong.

When you see how hard I am struggling, Teacher, please help me; don't yell, for I can't get anything right then.

When I pass a note in class, Teacher, please don't read it out aloud. Would you want me to find one of your letters and read it to the class?

Respect me, Teacher, for what I have the ability to become, not what you think I am.

Don't judge me by the neighborhood that I live in; I, too, want to march in the mainstream of society.

Don't be so quick to put me in a room for students labeled learning disabled; there is nothing to reach for there. To have children call me "retard" is cruel, Teacher. Would you want this to happen to you, Teacher?

When I act up in class, take the time to find out what hurts inside, Teacher. Help me to find another way to express myself.

I am young, Teacher, but I, too, have problems. Take the time to listen to my problems. Don't always praise the children who wear pretty clothing or who do everything right. I, too, want you to find something to say about me that is good.

I know that I get into trouble a lot, Teacher, but please listen to my side too. The more you listen, the less trouble I will get into. I need your respect. I love you, Teacher. I know that I don't always act as if I love you, but I do, Teacher.

I can't buy you Christmas presents, Teacher, but I love you too. Please encourage me to write you a note, and praise my note as much as you do Johnny's prettily wrapped Christmas present. If you teach me, Teacher, one day I will be able to buy you many Christmas presents.

Don't ask me to write what I am thankful for at Thanksgiving just because you have been patient enough to teach me, Teacher. I am not thankful; I am miserable. Help me, Teacher, to be thankful before Thanksgiving time arrives.

When I share my secrets with you, Teacher, please don't tell them to everyone. I will never trust you again. Tell me that you are proud of me, Teacher—honestly; I will live up to it.

I can learn anything, Teacher, if you will just give me a

chance. It may take me a little longer, but please tell me: "I have as much time as it takes. Don't worry, together we will get it right."

Don't tell me that I will never be anything, Teacher, for then I will find every excuse not to come to school each day. Tell me that you missed me when I am absent, Teacher, then I will make every effort to come to school.

Write a special note just to me, Teacher. I don't get much mail at my house.

Remain calm, Teacher, when I am upset; remember that you have had more practice with life than I have had.

Be the one person, Teacher, that does not yell, scream, or misunderstand me. I will become the person God meant me to be with your help.

7.
Beatitudes For Those Who Are Afro-American

Blessed are those of us who are self-motivated, self-generated, and self-propelled.

Blessed are those of us who go down roads armed with our own vision, knowing that we may fight, suffer, pay, but we will win.

Blessed are those of us who realize that those who ride the back of the tiger end up inside the tiger's mouth.

Blessed are those of us who realize that kites fly highest with the winds at our backs. Hard times do not always last; but tough people do.

Blessed are those of us who made our dreams a reality and who tenaciously dare to water and cultivate new and young dreams for those who must come after us.

Blessed are those of us who honor our ancestors by pursuing excellence every day, every moment, every second, realizing that excellence is a habit, not an act.

Blessed are the positive parents who rear positive children to honor their ancestors with acts of heroism and excellence.

Blessed are those of us who are empathetic with those of us who have lost the way, knowing that someone gave us a push to the top of the mountain of excellence.

Blessed are those who lead our children down paths of compassion, caring, hope, and love, knowing that one day our children will lead us.

Blessed are our teachers who take those children whom others declare lumps of coal and make them shining diamonds.

Blessed are our schools that take in the huddled masses destined to fail and show them success.

Blessed are our churches that realize that the people who do not attend church are often the ones most in need of compassion and help.

Blessed are our neighborhoods that bind up the hurting wounds of our children by becoming a united bandage that balms and soothes them.

Blessed are the nations, communities, townships, villages, and homes that know us, for we are excellent; won't you too, join our quest?

8

21 Memos From Your Child

1. Don't spoil me. I know quite well that I ought not to have all that I ask for. I am only testing you.

2. Don't be afraid to be firm with me. I prefer it; it makes me feel more secure.

3. Don't let me form bad habits. I have to rely on you to detect them in the early stages.

4. Don't try to make me feel smaller than I am. It only makes me behave stupidly "big."

5. Don't correct me in front of other people if you can help it. I'll take much more notice if you talk quietly with me in private.

6. Don't make me feel my mistakes are sins. It upsets my sense of values.

7. Don't protect me from consequences. I need to learn the painful way sometimes.

8. Don't be too upset when I say "I hate you." It is not you I hate but your power to thwart me.

9. Don't take too much notice of my small ailments. Sometimes they get me the attention I need.

10. Don't nag. If you do, I shall have to protect myself by appearing deaf.

11. Don't forget that I cannot always express myself as well as I would like. This is why I am not always very accurate.

12. Don't make rash promises. Remember that I feel badly let down when promises are broken.

13. Don't tax my honesty too much. I am easily frightened into telling lies.

14. Don't be inconsistent. That completely confuses me and makes me lose faith in you.

15. Don't tell me that my fears are silly. They are terribly real and you can do much to reassure me if you try to understand.

16. Don't put me off when I ask questions. If you do, you will find that I stop asking and seek information elsewhere.

17. Don't ever suggest that you are perfect or infallible. It gives me a great shock when I discover that you are neither.

18. Don't ever think it is beneath your dignity to apologize to me. An honest apology makes me feel surprisingly warm toward you.

19. Don't forget that I am growing up. It must be very difficult to keep pace with me, but please do try.

20. Don't forget that I love experimenting. I couldn't get along without it, so please put up with it.

21. Don't forget that I can't thrive without lots of understanding love, but I don't need to tell you, do I?

The Ten Teaching Commandments

1. Thou shalt love thy students as you would love your own children.

2. Do unto your students as you would have them do unto you.

3. Honor your students; praise as well as criticize.

4. Thou shalt not spend so much time being a teacher that you have forgotten what it is like to be a child.

5. Love your students so well that you give your last iota of energy to make them good citizens.

6. Thou shalt not let any students fail.

7. Thou shalt never give busy work.

8. Thou shalt never consider yourself in the Land of the Done. You, as a good teacher, know that you'll always strive to become a better teacher.

9. Thou shalt love freely, purely, consistently, and that love will return to you ten-fold.

10. Thou shalt respect every child and every parent, and always be true to the Latin meaning of the word *teacher*, which means "to lead or draw out."

9.
Readings That Help Me Through Bad Times

Problem: If I lost everything I had. . .

Solution: "If you can see the things you've given your life to broken and stoop and build them up again with worn-out tools and never breathe a word about your loss." (From the poem *If* by Rudyard Kipling)

Problem: When wanting to give up after a strenuous battle. . .

Solution: "I've waded too far in this bloody mess to turn back now." (From Shakespeare's *Macbeth*)

Problem: When fearful about a decision. . .

Solution: "Cowards die many times before their deaths; the valiant only taste of death but once." (From Shakespeare's *Julius Caesar*)

Problem: When disappointed in an action by someone I trusted. . .

Solution: "When I awaken, I say I will meet with the ingrate, the untrustful one. If they let me down, it's my misconception of them." (From Marcus Aurelius' *Meditations*)

Problem: When everything seems lost. . .

Solution: "Much was taken, but much still abides. To seek, to find, but never to yield. (From a poem, Longfellow's *Ulysses*)

Problem: When tempted not to keep my promise. . .

Solution: "We must pay the piper." (From the *The Pied Piper of Hamelin*)

Problem: When I would enter the public school where I taught for 14 years. . .

Solution: "Abandon all hope that enters here." (From Dante Alighiere's *Divine Comedy*)

Problem: On the power of God. . .

Solution: "Write me as one who loves my fellow-man." (From the poem, *"Abou Ben Adhem"*)

Problem: On believing in myself. . .

Solution: "Trust thyself, every heart vibrates to that iron string." Or. . .Polonious' advise to his son, Laertes: "To thine own self be true, and it must follow as the night the day, you cannot then be false to any man." (From Ralph Waldo Emerson's *Self-Reliance*)

Problem: When my dog will not leave the room. . .

Solution: "Out, out, damned Spot." (From Shakespeare's *Macbeth*)

Problem: When revealing my love. . .

Solution: "How do I love thee, let me count the ways." (From Elizabeth Barrett Browning's "43rd Sonnet")

Problem: When people attempt to outwit me and then become angry when they cannot. . .

Solution: "Two minds in control are inimical to good steering." (From Aeschylus)

Problem: When I see bad schools. . .

Solution: "Education is cumulative, and it affects the breed." (From Plato's *The Republic*)

Problem: When something smells badly. . .

Solution: "All the perfumes in Arabia could not sweeten this smell." (From Shakespeare's *Macbeth*)

Problem: When people are awed by brilliant people. . .

Solution: "Beware of Cassius, for Cassius is a lean man. Lean men are thinking men, and thinking men are dangerous." (From Shakespeare's *Julius Caesar*)

Problem: When people blame fate for what happens to them or seek answers from their horoscopes. . .

Solution: "Our fate is not within the stars, it is within ourselves." (From Shakespeare's *Julius Caesar*)

Problem: When I am accused of criticizing public schools. . .

Solution: "Not that I love the public schools less, I love our children more." (From Shakespeare's *Julius Caesar*)

Problem: When I am excessively flattered. . .

Solution: "Beware of idle words." (From the poem, "Spider and the Fly")

Problem: When I am extremely tired. . .

Solution: "I have miles to go, and promises to keep before I sleep." (From Robert Frost's poem, "Stopping by Woods")

Problem: When I am asked why I turned down the President's offer of a Cabinet post as Secretary of Education. . .

Solution: "I have taken the road seldom taken, and I hope to leave a path." (From Robert Frost's poem, "The Road not Taken")

Problem: When people attempt to convince me of their love and trust. . .

Solution: That's what Brutus told Julius Caesar, too. (From Shakespeare's *Julius Caesar*) Or that's what Delilah told Samson, too. (From the story of Samson and Delilah in the Bible)

Problem: When critics criticize my efforts to educate our children. . .

Solution: "God looks at the blank sheets of people more severely than he does the scribbled ones." (From Mother Theresa)

Problem: When I see the terrible things our children do because of mis-education. . .

Solution: "Confusion has made its masterpiece." (From Shakespeare's *Macbeth*)

Problem: When a friend betrays you. . .

Solution: "That was the unkindest cut of all." (From Shakespeare's *Julius Caesar*)

Problem: When told what young children cannot learn. . .

Solution: I reread John Stuart Mills' "Grasp of Latin," written at age 9, and Bach's compositions at age 4.

Problem: On something for free. . .

Solution: "Beware of Greeks bearing gifts." (From *The Iliad* by Homer)

Problem: When I am criticized for working too hard. . .

Solution: "Some people work themselves away; some people rust away." (From Epictetus' essay *On the Order of Things*)

Problem: When told that children are learning disabled. . .

Solution: "Abraham Lincoln has pen in hand, and he'll be good, but only God knows when." (From *The Story of Abraham Lincoln*. . .Abraham Lincoln learned to read at age 14 with *Aesop's Fables*.)

Problem: When someone who has died is criticized. . .

Solution: "The good that men do is often interred with their bones, while the evil lives long after them." (From Shakespeare's *Julius Caesar*)

Problem: When people predict my downfall. . .

Solution: "The witches predict, but only Macbeth and God can determine." (From Shakespeare's *Macbeth*)

Problem: The problems confronting a leader. . .

Solution: "Uneasy lies the head that wears a crown." (From Shakespeare's *Henry IV,* Part 2)

Problem: On life and death. . .

Solution: "Wc cach have our exits and our entrances." (From Shakespeare's *"Hamlet")*

Problem: When my enemies are after me. . .

Solution: "He prepareth a table before me in the presence of mine enemies." (From the 23rd Psalm)

Problem: When tempted to criticize others. . .

Solution: "Before getting the splinter from your neighbor's eye, get the plank from your own." (From The Bible)

Problem: On classes of people. . .

Solution: "We don't need further endless fragmentations of exclusivities of white men, black men, red men. We need men to answer the sad calls of humanity." (From Dr. Tom Dooley's letter to a young doctor)

Problem: When my individualism is questioned. . .

Solution: "The bigger the crowd the more negligible the individual becomes." (From C. G. Jung's *The Undiscovered Self)*

Problem: When discussing problems confronting our youth today. . .

Solution: "Hopes enunciated and principles expressed are not enough; we need people of action." (From Dr. Tom Dooley's Letter to a young doctor)

Problem: When frustrated by today's miseducation. . .

Solution: "Education was not designed for all people, but to take only a few to great and lasting heights." (From Friedrich Nietzsche)

Problem: People who want success, but are not willing to pay the price. . .

Solution: "Success gained and kept was not attained by sudden flight, but these people worked and toiled while others slept throughout the night." (From Aristotle)

Problem: On good and bad. . .

Solution: "Good and bad are but names very readily transferable to this or that." (From Shakespeare)

Problem: On the homeless. . .

Solution: "Let me live in a house by the side of the road, and be a friend to man." (From Walter Foss' "House by the Side of the Road")

Problem: On self-pride and determination. . .

Solution: "My head is bloody, but unbowed. I'm the captain of my fate; I'm the victor of my soul." (From William E. Henley's "Invictus")

Problem: On following our own thoughts and ideas. . .

Solution: "The mass of men lead lives of quiet desperation." (From Henry David Thoreau's *Walden*)

Problem: On getting angry. . .

Solution: "Men boil at different degrees." (From Henry

David Thoreau)

Problem: Curtailing individualism. . .

Solution: "If a man does not keep step with his companions, maybe it is because he hears a different drummer. Let him step to the drummer that he hears." (From Henry David Thoreau)

Problem: When losing sense of purpose. . .

Solution: Think of Odysseus in the *Odyssey* and his stalwart sense of purpose.

Problem: When problems seem insurmountable. . .

Solution: The story of Job (From the Bible)

Problem: When meeting a duplicitous person. . .

Solution: "Look like the innocent flower, but be the serpent under it." -or- "There are daggers in men's smiles." (From Shakespeare's *Macbeth*)

Problem: When my students do not listen. . .

Solution: "Boys and girls, lend me your ears." (From Shakespeare's *Julius Caesar*)

Problem: When I see problems in American society, today. . .

Solution: Gibbon's *Rise and Fall of the Roman Empire*

Problem: When politicians make promises. . .

Solution: Machiavelli's *The Prince*

Problem: When I wonder if my efforts for my students are worth the trouble. . .

Solution: "My father gave me life, but Aristotle [his teacher] taught me how to live it." (From Alexander the Great—Socrates taught Plato, Plato taught Aristotle, and Aristotle taught Alexander the Great.)

Problem: When we get new students, the first thing we have to teach them is the school's motto which is. . ."There are no free rides."

Solution: John F. Kennedy's speech, "Ask not what your country can do for you, but what you can do for your country."

Problem: When I need to laugh. . .

Solution: I read Petronious' *Satyricon*, Rabelais, and Chaucer's *Wife of Bathe*.

Problem: When I become too idealistic, I read. . .

Solution: Plato's *Republic* and Sir Thomas More's "Utopia."

Problem: When I hear people ridiculing Sages' predictions. . .

Solution: I read *Nostradamus*.

Problem: When failing in an endeavor. . .

Solution: Edison's statement about 123 failures when inventing the light bulb: "I know that there are 123 ways not to do it." (From Thomas Edison)

Problem: When criticized. . .

Solution: "Don't try to please everyone, for you'll please no one, not even yourself." (From Aesop's "The Man and the Donkey")

Problem: When criticizing one class of people or another. . .

Solution: "All things great and small, the Lord God loveth and made them all." (From Samuel Coleridge's *Ancient Mariner*)

Problem: On being real. . .

Solution: "Real only happens when you are frayed and torn. It doesn't happen to people who have been carefully kept. But, once you are real, you can never become unreal again. It lasts forever." (From *The Velveteen Rabbit*, by Marjorie Williams Bianco)

Problem: On that which is difficult. . .

Solution: Badness you can get in great quantity. The road to excellence is difficult and steep all the way. Once you reach the top, it is easy though it was hard. (From Comenius)

Problem: Going through difficult times. . .

Solution: "In a world that tosses all of us about and puts all sorts of questions to us, we must learn to steel the will in pleasure and in pain to do what must be done." (From The Great Books "Essay on Courage")

Problem: When the system tries to kill my will. . .

Solution: "Kill by laughter and ridicule." "Rule a man's soul and he is yours. Make him feel quietly, kill his aspirations and his integrity and will; and he won't need a whip— he will bring it to you and ask to be whipped." "Kill man's sense of values, kill his capacity to recognize greatness or to achieve it, and you will have the man." "Great men can't be ruled. Destroy a great architect, and you have destroyed architecture." "Empty a man's soul and will, and the space is yours to fill." (From Ayn Rand's *The Fountainhead*)

Problem: Individualism. . .

Solution: "The hardest thing in the world is to be me in a world where everybody is like everybody else." (From E. E. Cummings)

Problem: When hurt. . .

Solution: "It is not what happens to us, but our view of what happens to us." (From Epictetus' *The Manual*)

Problem: When far too many visitors visit our school. . .

Solution: "The unexamined life is not worth living." (From Socrates)

Problem: When students say, "I can't.". . .

Solution: "Remove the *t* from *can't,* and we have *can.* " (From Marva Collins)

Problem: When I feel unhappy or sad. . .

Solution: Dr. Robert Schuller's *The Be Happy Attitudes*

Problem: When politicians speak of public service. . .

Solution: "Where there is service, there is someone being served." "Where there is sacrifice, there are sacrificial offerings." (From Ayn Rand's *The Fountainhead*)

Problem: Miseducation in today's schools. . .

Solution: "Most schools are a perfect antithesis of the mockery of freedom." (From Ayn Rand's *The Fountainhead*)

Problem: Uniformed miseducation. . .

Solution: "Uniformed miseducation makes one neck for one leash. This defies individualized progress. It makes for mass failure." (From Ayn Rand's *The Fountainhead*)

Problem: When asked why I am so sincere about my efforts with inner-city children. . .

Solution: "Surely only a few children of any race will truly grasp the *real* meaning of education, and the reality of their potentials. It is the few however, who will give life its meaning—and it is those few for whom I have unselfishly exerted myself as one single sunbeam can chase away many shadows. May each of my students become lengthened shadows of my efforts." (From Ayn Rand's *The Fountainhead*, and *Atlas Shrugged*)

Problem: Problems confronting Blacks today.

Solution: *Let the Trumpet Sound* (The story of Dr. Martin Luther King, Jr.) by Stephen Oates.
Soul of Black Folks by W. E. B. DuBois
Life of Frederick Douglas by Frederick Douglas
Letter from a Birmingham Jail by Dr. Martin Luther King, Jr.
King Remembered, The Life of Dr. King by Schillke/Mc-Phee
Thunder in America (The Biography of Jesse L. Jackson) by Bob Faw

10.
Good Morning Children, Good Morning to You

I just came to have a few words with you.

In a world seemingly gone crazy you surely must wonder, "What would I do?"

Those who believe in you, my dark-skinned child, are very few.

I can understand why you feel so blue.

We watch the night news;

The missiles kill and maim

And you wonder, what's the aim?

Is it for power or for gain. . .

Is it for aggressor fame.

Meanwhile, innocent people are dying just the same.

While those of us here at home—

The homeless, victims of AIDS, poverty and miseducation—are too,

In real pain

Meanwhile we fight a war afar

And yet at home our dreams go astray

For the want of hitching them to a star.

You are taught, "Thou shalt not kill"

But killing is okay when our leaders send us afar to maim.

This must surely leave on your soul a hypocritical stain.

The sun sometimes struggles after a storm,

But still it appears.

Great music, great art often are borne out of severe pain.

We learn to fight to win

For what others tell us is patriotic pride

But amidst a carpet of glass and broken dreams at home,

Failure is always at our side;

The gap between the haves and the have-nots is still very wide.

Should you survive the slings and arrows of war,

You will return as an alien to a country where survival is often denied.

You are told protection of the American Dream must be your goal;

In reality, when you return to your native land, you will find the same old American nightmare.

You will find that those you have shed your blood for

In distant lands and in desert sands

Will not even shake your hand

America, we say, is fighting for freedom

But just dare to speak that word and you will find your muffled voice goes unheard. . .

In foreign lands we gave all that we had only to return to your homeland and hear. . ."You are bad. . .you are mad. . ."

In the words of Isaiah, "When we dare to say, Undo the heavy burdens of racism and callousness and let my people go. . ."

Utter these words and society proclaims us a foe.

Will you for once these simple words heed?

In the words of Shylock the Jew, "When pricked, do we too, not bleed?"

Would you, or our adversarial brothers, not feel pain

If you knew what you have your life for brought you no gain?

For once, may the long-locked rusty hearts in America

Begin to let just a little of your mercy season justice?

We too sing America.

We too yearn to walk in the light of freedom.

We too suffer from oppression.

We too choke on the leftover crumbs of society.

We too sigh.

We too cry.

We too dream.

We too aspire.

We too love life.

We too tire of strife.

Real freedom is never mired in a life.

Society, your continued alienation of our dreams, our desires diminishes each of us. . .

We too, your darker brothers and sisters, are pieces of the continent. . .

Our tyrannical brothers cease asking, "For whom the bells toll. . ."

They toll to make you see. . . .

That I too am dying to be free.

"A child who finds a teacher who believes in him is like a tree stripped bare of its leaves and fruits by a harsh winter. Gentle spring comes and gives life again."

11

Good Teacher is a Gentle Spring

A student is like a tree. Teachers who spend more time talking about what children should know and what they cannot do are delaying the time when that child's leaves can once again come into fruition. Surely the harsh winter of some teachers may be the culprit, but pointing fingers won't help the child who sits before you.

This child will constantly be at risk in society until somewhere someone sees him or her as a blank sheet of paper on which the good teacher will do the writing. The good teacher gives children the opportunity to have their past failures burned. They are given a new lease on life. . .a new opportunity to have the past die, never to be born again.

Caring cannot be forced; it must come of its own accord. When a teacher cares enough to keep polishing, the shiny luster that all children have comes shining through. Think for a moment about going into an antique shop where one views old silver. One person sees blackened metal and calls it worthless. Another viewer sees the blackened silver and realizes what it can become. With polishing, the true, fine luster comes shining through. The same silver existed all the time. The only difference is how the viewer saw its value and potential. So it is with children. Without vision of what a child can become, his potential perishes.

The good teacher removes the layers of dead leaves left from a harsh winter of uncaring and gives the child the sweet breath of spring. . .a new life. Spring itself means new beginnings. . .new life.

12.
You are Your Child's
First Teacher

Teaching Your Child to Read

Read something to your child each day. Then ask the following questions: Who did I read about? What happened in the story? Where did the story take place? What do you think will happen next?

Play vowel games with your child. Example: Say words such as cat, bat, fig, pot, pat, pet, rid, red, rut, hot, cap, etc. and have the child figure out which vowel is in each word. You not only teach your child to read but how to speak better.

Cut simple pictures from a catalog or magazine and have your child label and spell the names of the pictures.

Find a special place in your home (kitchen table or a dresser top) and leave daily worksheets for your child to complete. Find 30 minutes a day to spend with your child completing these sheets. Always make learning a top priority.

Use a dictionary to teach your child three new words a day. Remember, vocabulary is important for good readers. Do not allow your children to use the same words to describe things day after day. Instead of saying "big" constantly, supply the words "huge," "gargantuan," "gigantic," or "enormous" from time to time.

Remember, the time that you invest in your child's learning is also learning time for you. Teach your child colors and reading at the same time by saying, "These are your red socks." Then spell out the word "red." Say, "These are your R.E.D. socks." Do this for each item of clothing as your child is getting dressed.

Whatever your child learns to read, also have him learn to spell. Babies can learn to read by putting words on cards with pictures. Repeat the words to the child daily and show him the pictures, then remove the pictures and the child will soon say and spell the words without picture clues. THIS MUST BE DONE DAILY!

When you are cooking, ask the child to tell you the first letter in the word "pot" or "ham" or "steak" (or whatever you are cooking).

Read positive stories to your child which will instill values and teach morals. *The Velveteen Rabbit* teaches a lesson on becoming real. *Petunia* teaches the importance of learning to read and thinking for yourself. *The Pied Piper of Hamelin* teaches the importance of keeping your word. The story of *Pierre* teaches children to care about life. Read the poem *If* to teach determination. Consult our reading list for more titles. Read to your child no matter how old he is. Adolescents need and often want you to read with them or have them read to you. You then discover their strengths and weaknesses.

Discipline

When you must reprimand your child, do so in a loving manner. Don't every try to degrade or humiliate him. His ego is a precious thing worth preserving. Try saying:

I love you very much but I will not have that kind of behavior.

Do you know why I won't tolerate that? Simply because you are too bright to behave that way.

Whenever a child does something positive, always take the time to say, "I am so proud of you, bright boy or girl."

When a child makes a mistake, never call him stupid; simply say "let's proofread this" or "very good try."

When the child has a temper tantrum, say to the child, "I don't know that person who is acting out right now, but I am sure my bright, well-behaved child will return very quickly now. So I'll just leave the room until he returns."

Whatever you do to discipline your child, it must be done

consistently. Many times we promise rewards for good behavior and never pay up—this teaches the child that your word cannot be trusted.

Involvement

Teach your preschool child shapes such as circles, squares, etc. You can buy inexpensive books in the supermarket to help you with this. The child who gets some help at home is always a step ahead when he goes to school. Raising a bright child is your first responsibility.

When shopping, make your child a helper. Ask him to bring you a pound of grapes. Ask if one pound cost $1.19, then how much will three pounds cost? A half a pound?

Have children count the steps as they ascend or descend. Always tell them they are so bright.

When you are cooking or cleaning, have the child help you. Even young children can be given chores to help teach responsibility. Give the child an allowance and help him learn to budget his money and save some too.

Be concerned with your child's school progress not only at report card time but each day. Ask, "What did you learn in school today?" And don't ever take "nothing" for an answer.

Play math games with your child. Ask what number comes before three but after one? Then do four plus six, minus two equals what? Increase the difficulty according to the age of the child.

Teach your child to be a good listener by giving him a series of words or numbers and ask him to repeat the series and add on two words or numbers at the end.

Play rhyming words with your child.

When you are driving, have him count the cars and buildings, and have him give you a total when you arrive at your destination. Teach him to categorize things, e.g. how many stone buildings? How many churches? How many red cars?

Insist on correct English and complete sentences from your child. Children write the same way that they speak.

13.

I Am Failure

I am failure. I am as ancient as time. I ask nothing of you, and my streets are easy all the way. You never have to go to school, you never have to worry about time, and everything you touch is simple. I demand nothing of you, and you pay no dues to belong to my club of failure. All you have to do to belong to the club of failure is to be filled with excuses, sleep all day, steal, maim, kill, rob, and have no conscience. You will find my members in church, school, and jails, on the street, and in your neighborhood. You can always tell me because I have a swagger to my walk. I am filled with talk of great things I am going to do one day, but right now I do nothing. I live in the worst areas of the city, I drive the worst car, and live in the worst homes. I am low-self-esteem, I am hopeless. . .I am despair. . .I am failure.

14.
A Child's Plea

He always wanted to say something, but the teacher never understood. The children would laugh, so he just sat there, and in time he was like a bulb that never came on again. He hated school. He hated the militaristic rows and the papers that everyone did just alike. He hated it when the teacher said, "Why can't you do as well as Joe?"

He was not Joe; he was unique. Couldn't the teacher understand that? The teacher never really knew him; why did she pretend that all he ever did was daydream every time his mother came to inquire about his progress? Why couldn't the teacher ever say that she cared more about me paying attention and learning than my feet being flat on the floor? Why couldn't the teacher tell my parents that she never valued my thoughts, and that I always had to write about what she wanted me to write about? Why didn't she ever tell my mother that there was no place for me to go—I had already learned too thoroughly that I couldn't do anything right. Where does one go when he has repeatedly failed? Couldn't you, Teacher, have just told me once, "This is good, but let's look at this."

Those red marks on my paper—everything is wrong; why should I try again? You have taught me, Teacher, that I am a failure. You have measured my intelligence, Stanined my soul, and ink-blotted my future. . .what is left for me to do? My paper is always graded *sloppy, you can do better*, or *poor*. Why can't you for once try to help me correct my errors before I finish my paper? My mistakes are all too much for me to correct when the entire page is already wrong.

Were you never a child, Teacher? Did you never make mistakes? Did you always do everything right? Were you born a grown-up? The best day of my life, Teacher, is Saturday, because that is the one day that I don't have to hear all the things that are wrong with me. Saturday is the only day that I can do anything right. Teacher, how would you feel if you had to go home with a report card I had given you, and have your family ridicule you about how dismal your failures were? Would you feel good, Teacher?

Remember, when I try to hurt you, Teacher, it is only because you have hurt me so much and I am only trying to make you feel some of the hurt that I have inside me. It hurts so badly, Teacher, when you never call upon me to read, when you never praise me, when you ignore me—that hurts, Teacher. Please try to like me the way you like Joe, Amy, Ann, and Bob. I try, Teacher, but please touch me sometimes, too. You never pay attention to me until I have done something to displease you. Help me to be able to please you, Teacher. Help me to grow up in this world and not hate myself and my world because I feel that everyone sees me as a failure the way you do, Teacher. I am yours, Teacher. Help me; it is your duty to teach me to love myself, my world, and yes, to like school. I beg you, Teacher, please!

15

Excellence the Marva Collins' Way: A Collection of Poetry and Essays

I Am Excellence

I bear the flame that enlightens the world. I fire the imagination. I give might to dreams and wings to the aspirations of men.

I create all that is good, stalwart and long-lasting. I build for the future by making my every effort superior today.

I do not believe in "can't" or "might-have been."

When society draws a circle that will shut me out, I will design my own circle that will draw me in.

I am the parent of progress, the creator of creativity, the designer of opportunity, and the molder of human destiny.

Because of me, man holds dominion over himself, his home, his community and his world. I leash the lightening and plumb the ether.

From out of the shadows of the past I come wearing the scars of mistakes made by others. Yet I wear the wisdom and contributions of all ages. I dispel yesterday's myths and find today's facts. I am ageless and timeless.

I have no time for vice, crime and destruction. I banish mediocrity and discourage being average. I can function in pleasure or in pain. I can steel the will to do what must be done. Fortunate are the individuals, communities and nations that know me.

Men and the world are my workshops. Here I stir ambition, forge ideals and create the keys that open the door to worlds never dreamed. Earth awakes unfolding to me. Life is always calling me. My greatest success is yet to be discovered.

I am the source of creation, the outlet of inspiration, the dream of aspiration. I am excellence. Won't you, too, light my candle? Don't let me flicker away!

Ain't Got Time

I ain't got time to shed no tears
I will be gone in a few years
I have no time to cry
There are just too many things to try
And too many children to save before I die.
I ain't got no time to talk back to you
I have just too much to do before I die.
I must teach our children to fly
Teach them to be un-programmable,
To be in command, and teach our black boys to be men
So I ain't got time to talk back to you
There is just too much for me to do
Successes for our children are just all too few
And too many of our people are poor and blue
And so you see, I ain't got no time to talk back to you
There is just too much to do.

Had We Been. . .We Too

Had we been a dishonest people, we never could have been fooled away from our native land
For dishonesty never sleeps
Had we been a violent people, you never could have caught me
And today I would be free
Had we been liars, we could have fooled you
We are a tired, proud people and oh so. . .so disgusted and
So tired of living with a carpet of glass instead of a carpet of grass
We are so tired of hope being a yellow sheet flapping over a dismal alley
Can't you understand
That we too, want dignity in this land
Just a chance to prove that we too, can be a man
We are tired of being stuck in worthless sand
While you rule the land
Proving more and more that I am not a man
All we ask is justice as a demand
To prove too, that we are tired of your plan
I, too, want to be a man.

Inspiration
July 23, 1983

I am in danger, teacher; you rescue me.

I say things when I am angry, Teacher, and you forgive me for you know that I hurt inside.

I am in the dark, Teacher, and you show me light.

I am doubtful and you give me faith.

I am neglected, and you teach me.

You ignore the tags, labels and the former statistics that have signified that I am a failure. . .you show me success.

I am a child, and you show me the way. You know that I still have to grow, to learn, and to become.

You know that I can be more than what I am, and you are patient enough to never give up on me.

Everybody else says that I am "bad," but you, Teacher can see the "good" me, and for you I become good.

I am lost and you give me directions.

I waste time and you show me how to use my time wisely.

You do not nag. . .you forgive. . .and you show me that you care not just by the things you say to me, but I see the love for me in your eyes and I dare not let you down. . .

I succeed, Teacher for you, and before I know it I have learned to love success.

I see only today, but you show me the vision of the future.

You make me like what I see in the future, and therefore I am motivated to use today more wisely.

When I attempt to go backwards, you push me forward.

I am sometimes stunted by the failures of my past, and you make me see the glory of the future.

You have unblocked my fetid channels through which now creativity and self-reliance can flow.

You see today as my beginning, and you do not remember the decadent past.

When I am afraid, you give me courage. . .when I am marooned by the problems of life, you encourage me to steel the will in pleasure or in pain to go forth. I want to learn. . .I want to achieve. . .and you teach me.

Thank you, Teacher. Know what? I love you.

I love you because you are so forgiving. I love you because when the world saw failure, you, Teacher, saw light. Because of you that light shall never flicker, and I am now motivated to light the dying embers of others who too, have been tagged and labeled. Never forget, Teacher. . .I love you.

Teacher To Child

Child, don't you stop trying to learn because someone tells you that you will never amount to anything.

Don't you pay attention until you find your own light

Remember all men and women must raise themselves by their own might

And not by what is wrong or right

In the eyes of others who insist on telling you that life is an empty plight

Remember the slaves who learned to read and write in the night

Why then can't you find your way in the light?

Every man and woman has a place divinely given

Stand up and shout with all your might:

"This is my time and my place!" I will stand up and shout: "Don't you count me out!"

Take those frowns from your face

Child don't you let anyone take you from the race:

You have no time to waste

Trying to find the spot given you by someone else as your place

You, child, must find your own space.

Thousands will tell you that it cannot be done, thousands will tell you that you are bound to fail,

That the only place that awaits you is jail,

But only you, child, know how far you can sail,

So say to yourself, "You may predict, but I will not fail."

There will be times when you feel that all is up

That life has drained itself from your cup,

But heart within and God overhead,

Child, don't you give up.

Time and chance comes to every man,

Don't miss your chance child because someone said, "Are you sure?"

Of course, you can.

Remember always you are as good as any man
Wherever they may be on this land
Learn to take your life into your own hand
And then say, "I will, and I can."
The people who yell the loudest, "You can't"
Are usually the people who rave and rant
That it cannot be done
But child, you can be the one
Who did not stop until the things they said couldn't be
done
Were done. . .show the world that you will be the one
Who did the things that others said couldn't be done.

Marva Collins
by William Walker

There is an heroic woman
Whose story I'm eager to tell,
Who refused to teach school anywhere
Unless she could teach it well.
But that wasn't permitted in government schools,
So she started one of her own;
And with only the help of her husband,
She tore into the job alone
She had to accept the rejects. . .
The children considered unteachable;
But Marva Collins knew in her heart
That all of these children were reachable.
It wasn't an easy thing to repair
The mistakes of the mediocrities,
But Marva Collins soon had those children
Quoting from Shakespeare and Socrates
And learning their arithmetic,
And learning how to behave;
And learning to believe in themselves,
And for learning itself to crave.
Disadvantaged? Not any more,
Thanks to some powerful aid!
And one can be sure that a teacher like Marva
Is the sunlight which banishes the shade.

Growing Strong

I was born in a dump
My mattress was an endless lump
Life was filled with pain and bumps
My mamma died and my daddy got drunk
He left me in misery to die or grow
I grew up in a rusty shack. . .
All I owned was a raggedy shirt on my hungry
back. . .
The Lord knows how I loathe
This place called home. . .
But it's all that I have
It's all I have ever known. . .
I am gonna blow up this place and start anew
With a place that's fit to grow
I will build a town that's fit to show
I will save another child from misery's blow
Dismal alleys. . .broken glass. . .sheets flapping
over
A carpet of glass. . .
Missing grass. . .
Learning to live fast. . .
And we call this civilization. . .
What humiliation?
Someday though I will grow rich. . .
I will grow strong. . .
And I will return and build a town
That will show society just how wrong
They have been
To have us live in filthy sin.

Caring Makes a Difference
May, 1988

Year after year we take in the
troubled ones. . .
Your sons and your daughters
Sometimes we never receive the gratitude
for all that we have done
These children have been labeled "misfits". . .
outcasts. . .the rising underclass
And with love, caring, and dedication,
we never let those labels last.
On the playground, in the classroom
We make your child feel that
we will be the one
To help him or her do all the things
others said couldn't be done.
No longer do your children have to feel
"What's wrong with me?"
We teach them to love themselves and then
they feel free
To be all that God meant them to be.
We know that learning must go beyond the three R's
of learning to read, count, and to write. . .
We believe that all children must first learn to be
acceptable in their own sight
And then they will always choose the right
We remove the undue pressures
of failure, and "I Can't"
We teach your children that they are unique
and special
They are free from the traditional mold and form
of failure and hopelessness
Because we teach them their own uniqueness
We teach them that they were not meant to be
like you or me. . .
To be all that God created them to be.

We never teach your children to simply survive
We teach them that helping themselves first, and
then others is truly the way to thrive
We give your children love and understanding
challenge and fun
And we teach them that they are the greatest
and most unique people under the sun
Though your children may be small
we teach them that their thoughts and contributions
are valued. . .and that their thoughts today
may benefit us all.
I wonder why others found it so hard
to understand that your children were not difficult
or hard to teach
We simply gave your children wings of self-esteem
and taught them how to dream
Your children have learned how to fly
And now their confidence is soaring high
As I watch your children go into the world so free
I watch the gifts I gave your children and I see
also some of me.
Teaching is such a lofty and rewarding goal. . .
Especially when I can see the lives of your children
truly unfold
And to know that I played a small role
In helping them reach life's goal.

Growing up Black in the
Red Hills of Alabama
January 30, 1991

You gave me your tattered books, old and worn
You gave me the worst buildings, cold and forlorn
You nurtured me the way snow nurtures a weed
and still I knew I had to succeed
You Stanined my soul, you inkblotted my mind
Light and Freedom was always hard to find
Despite the manacles and hardened reins
On books I would dine
I knew that I had to turn out fine
And I worked hard indeed
So that I could say, still I succeed.
You looked at me with a negative mind
Success you were so sure I would never find
The more you said I couldn't
The harder I tried
Just to show you that you could not look
At me like a seed
To tell which was a flower and which was a weed
Despite it all you see. . .I did succeed.
You said I would never come to any good
But I had to show you that I would
You see, you never understood
The fire in my chest
To show you that I would not be mired in
the red clay
Like all the rest
You put me to the failure test
But it was all for no need
For you see, I did succeed.
We were all told that being black assures you
that you will never do anything right
But I paid no attention, and I found my own light

You tried with all your might
To hold me down with your negative slight
Despite your doleful and intentional deed
You see, I did succeed.
I saw the negative frowns on your face
And this made me know that I had no time to waste
I had to find my own space
I had to outdistance the failure race
I had a burning need
You see, I had to succeed.

To Mike R.
June 30, 1989

Half a league, half a league
Half a league backward
All in the valley of illiteracy
Rode the massive hundreds
"Charge for the criminals," they said,
As into the valley of illiteracy
Rode the massive hundreds.
Backwards went the illiterate herd
There were many dismayed
Someone had blundered
Theirs not to make reply
Theirs but to fail and die
As into the valley of illiteracy
Rode the massive hundreds.
Drugs and crime to the right of them,
Failure and fetidness to the left of them,
Failure in front of them
Volleyed and thundered
Stormed at with statistics and more and
More reports of the failing underclass
But boldly they trudged the streets and well
Into the jaws of Hell and failure
Rode the massive hundreds.
Flashed all their criminal skills
Flashed as they fled through the fetid air
Sabring the criminal art
Charging back at society while
All the world wondered
Plunged into the criminal facilities until they
Were all filled
Right through the police lines they broke
Some were shattered and sundered
But then more were created and they rode back
Rode the new massive hundreds.

Crimes in front of them
Crimes in back of them
Crimes behind them
Stormed at with shot and shell
But the criminals knew their art too well
They laughed at the mouth of Hell
Oh! when will their failure fade?
Oh! what wild charges failure has made!
How shall we handle the failure Brigade?
(Adapted from "Charge of the Light Brigade" by Alfred
Lord Tennyson)

The Dropout

When as a child I'd always dream of the
things I would become someday
Somewhere there would be people who would care
People who would share
the dreams, aspirations, and goals that I had
Little did I realize that I would be labeled "bad."
As time went by I was a statistic that was
all too sad.
I went to class did the best I could
Never learned the things that I should
The brighter students had all the chances
Soon I learned to survive by acting out in class
I learned to be the class clown
This is how I drowned my sorrows and my pain
By making others laugh while I cried inside with
so much hurt and shame
I never learned to read, never learned to write,
I only learned how to fight
And fighting and hating I did with all my might.
Soon I decided to take to the streets to learn
to be mean
To be seen, to yell and scream. . .to hate and fight. . .
I was a desperate soul in flight
I dropped out of school
I was tired of being the class's fool
I was never taught the learning tool
And now I try to be so cool
Someday soon I hope someone will take my hand
And care, really care
And show me another way. I do want to learn
to read and write
Please help me in my plight
I, too, want to see the light.

Flight
May 27, 1987

Inner pain,
No relief in sight
No where to take flight
You hurt with all your might
To make the pain right
You toss and turn in the night
Trying to do what is right
Waiting for the dawn's light
To begin again another cycle of pain
That showers down like rain
Will laughter ever come again?

Validate Me
May 26, 1987

"You are wrong",
"You are too strong"
"That's not right"
"This is what you should do"
"Can't you see what we see in you?"
Please me
Do what I ask of you
Don't worry about pleasing yourself
Leave your own needs on a shelf
Who cares if your own life is bereft?
Validate me. . .
Help me to feel that I am free
I try so hard to please can't you see?
You never mention the things that I do
that are right.
You seem only to see those that you see
as wrong,
As I plod among the crowds and things
of people like you
I try so hard to do the things you want
me to do
And yet when we disagree
I only hear the side that is the bad me
The good things that I have done are
caged and left unfree
While I stand pleading for you to validate
me.
I love and care under all conditions
Because I feel that this is life's mission
My hand is the first to reach out
While many times you sit and pout
Did it ever occur to you that I, too, am blue
That there are times when I too, need you
I am the first to always say, "I love you"

The times I have heard these words have been all too few I hurt. . .I feel. . .I, too, need to be. . .

Won't you please validate me?
(Written for Kevin Ross)
May 28, 1987

Too many empty spaces
Too many callous faces
Too many thickened walls
That do not hear my frightened calls
Too many people who do not hear my painful wail
Too many people helping me fail
The walls just got too tall
Now I don't care at all.

Win! Win! Win! Win at any cost.
Losing is a sin
Show the world that you are boss
Win at any cost
When will we teach our children that losing too
is an art?

Untitled
May 27, 1987

Vacant spaces like vacant lots
often become a dumping ground
where love is never found. . .

Soul in Flight
Written for Kevin Ross
May 27, 1987

I slipped the surly reality of light
and now my soul is in flight
Lord, help me to do that which is right
Help me to regain favor in your sight
This I ask with all my might,
Bring me again to the ray of light
Retrieve my soul from the abysmal dark
I lost my way in the voyage of life
I gave in to the inner-strife
of pain that would not go away,
But Lord bring me home this day.
Show me Lord your way. . .I never
meant to go astray.

Nostalgia
(Written for Kevin Ross)
May 27, 1987

I saw my friend today
He had so many things to say
He told me of his wife and home and job
and then he turned to me,
"What about you?" He said
How does one respond? Should I tell him my life
is a mess
That I failed life's test?
Can't he look at me and guess the rest?
Four years of dunking the ball
No time to learn to read and write
And now with no skills
Where do I find a job?
Where do I pick up my lost self-esteem?
All is up for me it would seem
Sometimes the pain inside makes me want
to scream
I lost the American dream
The scoreboards are silent. . .the crowd has
gone away
and now I am left with just today
I look at my friends who have gotten on
with their life
and mine is filled with strife.

Making the Big Time
May 25, 1987

The college recruiters came in glee
Seeking the big-time athlete, me.
No one ever bothered to teach me
to read, write, or spell
And so. . .I assumed the contracts
I signed to be good and well.
Little did I know then I was signing
myself into Hell. . .
And all for the sound of the glory
bell.
I was about to conquer the world in
a pair of gym shoes
Or so I thought. . .it never dawned upon
me that I was going to be used
and tossed away like an old pair of
shoes.
Winning was all that mattered.
Never mind that our lives were being shattered.
Free alcohol flowed like a thunderous rain
This was to help ease any inner pain
Little did I know then that this was not gain
And that later my life would always bear the stain
Of being an illiterate in shame.
The experts picked my courses for me
And little did I know that I would never be free
Of going through life with no skill
And becoming a lifetime leaner with no will.
The crowds are silent now. The scoreboard
is no longer lit.
My gym shoes no longer fit.
I'm no longer interested in dunking the ball
I'm too busy trying to move this illiteracy wall
And so while others walk through life, I am forced
to crawl

For a fleeting moment of possible fame
I am now living in shame.
I hope the coaches who now recruit our youth
will only tell them the truth.
In my moments of gloom
I sit in my room
And I think of my present doom.
I look over the frayed and yellowed accolades
of what I might have been
And I am forced to look at the reality of the
mess my life is in
The pain becomes so severe that I wish I was
not here
I escape to find something to lessen the pain
and ease the shame
To think I sold my life for moments of fame
I gave my life for what might have been
And now look at the shape I am in.
Those recruiters who have boys of your own
I hope their hearts will never be torn
I hope some caring person will take their hand
And say, "Young man, it's fine to win, but low
aim; that is a sin."
I hope someone will tell your sons, "It's fine to
learn to dunk the ball. . .to have a fan. . .but
most of all learn the skills first that will
make you a man."

Lost Faith
May 28, 1987

He always believed he would be great one day
That life would not always be this way
Broken hopes, lost aspirations, broken promises,
Shattered dreams
Mommy said, "Go to school and you will learn. . .
You will become a great man one day."
But what Mommy never knew is that the teacher
screams all day
"Can I ever become great this way?"
"Sit down, shut-up," "Finish that sheet"
"Don't move until they are complete," she
yelled. When I tried to say, "But, Teacher
I don't understand," she yelled again,
"Sit down young man!"
Mommy said, "Go to school and pay attention; be
a good boy, and you will learn."
I tried to ask Mommy what I should do when
there was nothing to pay attention to.
we were only given cold mimeographed sheets
and became a part of a nuts-and-bolts crew
of trying to complete something we never learned
Does this mean that I will be caged into a cycle
of poverty for evermore?
Will my children, too, ask for bread
And I must answer, "I am sorry you can't be fed."
Will my children too one day wish that
they were dead
Because too many broken dreams gives them
hearts of lead
Must my children too, eternally wed
The crosses of poverty
My faith here on earth never came true
But maybe. . .maybe. . .maybe eternity?

Lonely in a World Filled With Too Many People
Videos, radios, television, movies, rock music
All the noise
And the laughter of the boys
Surely there is much to do
So why are you blue?
Microwaves, no time for family dinner
Only more time to become a winner
Only more time to become a sinner
Egos become weaker, and days and nights bleaker
Busy every moment, and yet I find I am
always behind
In things I meant to do, people I meant to see
Things I meant to say
Mountains I meant to climb. . .moments
I meant to find
And yet I sit alone and pine. . .I lie and say, "Life
is fine," and yet the pain inside hurts so
Where is there for me to go?
I wear the happy mask, and so
None dare ask
"Are you okay?" "How are you today?"
Lord make the loneliness go away. . .this to you
I pray.

I Blame Racism

I blame racism
Though racism exists
I still am the captain of my own fate
No racist comes to my house and dares me
to be all that I can be
No racist comes to my house and dares me to read
No racist comes to my house and defies me
to be excellent
I blame the single family home
Some homes are actually better
When the negative one is gone
And so that places the blame right back on me
I am the one that will make me free
I am responsible for being all that I can be
I blame the government
For not giving me all that I need
What I must see is that I am the weed
That keeps me from being the fragrant flower
That can be anything I want to be
No one knows my needs the way I do
And so, those needs must be supplied by me
And that is why I have the greatest equipment
That the greatest have had
Two eyes, a brain, two hands, two feet
If I am to be free and to succeed, I must use these
As the greatest have done
And then I, too, can say, "I won"
I blame my neighborhood
No one makes me go and hang on the corner
No one makes me take drugs
No one makes me not pick up a book
No one dares me enter the library
No one makes me not do my homework
No poor teacher can take away my right to be free

That freedom is left up to me.
I blame my parents
They can either become a stumbling block
or a stepping stone
I can pledge never to fail as they have done
Or I can be another failing one
To declare all the reasons why I never won.
I blame the system
I hate those who worked while I slept
I hate those who worked while I rested
I hate those who have all the things I desire
But never wanted to work, struggle, and pursue to
have those things too.

Recipe for Excellent Students
October 4, 1991

One class of children of all creeds, races, and colors.

Heaping doses of praise.

Daily doses of "You are bright, you can do it."

Plenty of "You children are a promise, a great bundle of potentiality."

Frequent reminders of "I will not let you fail."

Mix thoroughly with bright, motivated, positive teachers until the eyes of children hold wonder like a cup.

Nurture above children for a few years, and there will be ample servings for the locales of the world, for society, and with equal ease, these children will one day maintain the American dream.

The temperature should always be warm, caring, dedicated, and genuinely loving.

How Do I Love Thee?
October 4, 1991
(With apologies to Elizabeth Barrett Browning)

How do I love thee dear students?
Let me count the ways.
I love thee when you make mistakes for I know that
these mistakes will become stepping stones.
I love thee to the level of what you can become and
not for what you might have been.
I love you without constraints or conditions.
I love thee purely without the strings
of more and more statistics, doubts or failure.
I love thee with a love that grows each day
more powerful than the day before.
I love thee with the math, English, science,
literature, geography, and French
I manage to teach.
And if God chooses,
I shall but love thee even more
with each passing day.

16.
Knowledge

A creek of knowledge is not enough; why not venture into the wide ocean of infinite knowledge?

If you have cursed the darkness, make certain that you have lit a candle for the darkness of your time. . .

Do you wear the scars of your mistakes so that you are not doomed to repeat them. . .?

Is the classroom your workshop? Have you forged ideals and created your own keys that will forge your own future. . .?

Are you the outlet of aspiration for others. . .the source of creation. . .the dream of aspiration?

The stiff currents of life must never suck us in. . .we must learn to endure in pleasure or in pain the slings and arrows of life knowing that the world is our stage and we are all merely players, each having our exits and our entrances. . .

This too, shall pass away. Time and hour runs through the roughest day. . .

Cowards die many times before their deaths, the valiant only taste of death but once. . .

True thinking emancipates us from the whips and scorns of slavery

Intellectual slavery, forced failure. . .

Life must be a computing principle where we add, subtract, and multiply. . .we are the addends and what we do with our life is the total sum. . .if we subtract what we have left of our lives, is the difference. . .

We should have complained long ago of such failure—there would have been a time for such a word. . .but now tomorrow and tomorrow creeps in this petty place from day to day until the last syllable of recorded time. . .who, then has time anchored on excuses?

Who can succeed, fail, achieve and fail all at the same time? No man. Keeping this in mind we then must, with the determination of a lit firecracker and the tenacity of a steel trap, decide to carve our own lives from decayed trunks of life. . .

There has been a ceremony of the innocents in this land. . .the innocents have been us, the children. . .we have been abused, miseducated, spoken for and about. . .and now it is our turn. . .so friends, foes, and comrades, lend me your ears. . .I came to tell you of your wrongs, not to applaud your rights. . .you have told us that we are no good, that we cannot think. . .and as adults, you are honorable men. . .right? Wrong? Now let me speak.

17.

The Creed

Society will draw a circle that shuts me out, but my superior thoughts will draw me in.

I was born to win if I do not spend too much time trying to fail.

I can become a citizen of the world if I do not spend too many energies attempting to become a local.

I will ignore the tags and names given me by society since only I know what I have the ability to become.

I will continue to let society predict, but only I can determine what I will, can, or cannot do.

Failure is just as easy to combat as success is to obtain.

Education is painful and not gained with playing games, but I have seen failure too destroy millions with promised hopes and broken dreams.

While I have the opportunity I shall not sit on the sideline bitter with despair and wish later that I had become a literate lifter of this world instead of a failing leaner.

I will use each day to the fullest. I promise that each day shall be gained, not lost—used, not thrown away. Yet, it is my privilege to destroy myself if that is what I choose to do.

I have the right to fail, but I do not have the right to take my teacher and other people with me. God made me the captain of only one life. . .my own.

Therefore, if I decide to become a failure, it is my right.

We were all promised a pursuit of happiness, and that is what I must do, pursue happiness and success for myself. No one will give it to me on a proverbial platter, and no one will care as much about me as I must care about myself, but I must be willing to accept the consequences for that failure and I must never think that those who have chosen to work while I played, rested and slept will share their bounties with me.

I will wave proudly my flag signifying that I am a failure by choice, but I will never envy those who have selected to wave their unfurled banners announcing their success.

My success and my education can be a companion which no misfortune can depress, no crime can destroy, no enemy can alienate. No envy or names can hurt me.

Education and success can be a lifetime solace. It guides goodness, it gives, at once, grace and genius to governments, communities, cities, townships, villages, homes and palaces.

Without education what is a man? A splendid slave, a savage, a beast wandering from here to there believing whatever he is told.

God is not some cosmic bellboy that comes at my beck and call. If I want to achieve, the first step must be my undertaking. Likewise, if I want to fail, that, too, is my choice. Time and chance comes to us all, whether I decide to take that time and chance is indeed my own choice.

I can either be hesitant or courageous. . .life does indeed maroon the hesitant and inspire the brave.

I can swiftly stand up and shout: "This is my time and my place, I will accept the challenge!" or I will let others make my decisions for me.

18

The Habit of Winning

WINNING IS NOT A SOMETIME THING. YOU DON'T WIN ONCE-IN-A-WHILE. You don't do things right once-in-a-while. You do them right all the time.

Winning is a habit. Unfortunately, so is losing. There is no room for second place.

There is only one place in my game and that is first place. I have finished second twice in my time and I never want to finish second again. The second place in any game is for losers. It is and must always be your zeal to be first in anything that you do, and to win, and to win, and to win, but only by soaring with your own wings. Do not be afraid to lose so that you may dare to know how to win.

Every time you play to win you must use every inch of you. You have got to be smart in this world to win. Don't worry about the people who grin. If you always have a lot of head and a lot of heart you are never going to come in second.

The objective in life is to win by carrying your own load. This does not mean that you walk over others to reach your goal. You simply put your shoulders to the task and to not stop until you have done your best.

It is a reality in life that when you do something well you become a standard for the world. People will never worry about the average man. They only follow the man who shows that he knows how to lift his load and refuses to lift those who want to lean.

Any man is happier when he has done the best he could for a good cause. He knows his finest hour, his greatest fulfillment and all that he holds dear is inherent in what he knows he has given his best to.

Things will always go wrong in life as they often do,
The road will often seem difficult
And many will tell you, "It can't be done."
Don't give up the task with a sigh, but stick it out
even if the pace seems slow.
You will usually succeed with only another blow.
The goal is often nearer
When you feel like quitting.
The struggler never gives up
Until he has captured the victor's cup.
Hold your head up and work
until the night comes down.
You will soon be closer to the crown.
Success is usually failure in disguise
The silver tint of the clouds may only be doubt,
You will never know how close to winning you were
If you decide to give up.
Stick to the fight of life when it seems afar
Even when you are hardest hit.
You must win and never, never, never quit.

19.
I Am the Teacher

I am the teacher. . .I am as ancient as Jesus himself. . .or Socrates. . .I am more than ancient; I am eternal. . .I mold my students for the future by making today different. . .my classroom is a workshop where all children find the opportunity to give might to their brains. . .here they believe that they can plumb the ether and shackle the lightning. . .

When the first trees and flowers and grasses appeared I was here. . .I was the teacher who taught the universe the beauty of the trees. . .the fragrance of the flowers. . .It was my students' words that recorded the first history of mankind. . .When men and women are struggling to find the "good them". . .I influence them to never let the "bad them" conquer the good so that they will never have to go through life with fuzzy and blocked channels. . .in all ages and times I have inspired men and women with lofty thoughts. . .with determination. . .with perserverance. . .I make my students excited about the voyage of life. . .I refuse to have any of my students sit on the sidelines catching the crumbs of the mainstream. . .I hurt when my students hurt. . .I am sad when they are sad. . .I understand their private pain. . .I help them succeed despite many times their denial that they need my help. . .I do not believe in Stanine-ing. . .inkblotting and measuring my students. . .I believe that all of them can achieve if they are not taught too thoroughly that they cannot achieve. . .

20.
What Shall I Tell
My Students Who Are Poor?

What shall I tell my children who are poor?

Of what it means to be judged by where one lives?

What shall I tell my students who are the clay sculptured by my humble hands?

What shall I tell my students who did not grow under my heart, but whom I have allowed to enter my heart?

How can I ever tell my students how bright they are when everywhere they turn they see failure, fetidness, decadence, and statistics of how miserably they have failed?

How can I teach my students that hope does not have to be yesterday's scattered ashes or a dingy yellow sheet flapping over a dismal alley? The poor cannot travel, the poor never have enough of anything, not even dreams. The poor cannot make decisions. The poor are isolated into forgotten regions where conditions become more and more decadent, making way for those more verbal than they to speak for them.

What shall I tell my dear students raised in a world where everything that is good is given to the heirs of the rich? How shall I tell my students that they must begin to be the generic heirs that will make tomorrow different because, together, we dared to dream today?

What can I say to give my students strength, fortitude, perseverance, and the determination to rise above today's poverty and to reach out and touch another man who may have lost his way without their help? What shall I tell my students who are poor when the teacher's guide not once alludes to the hurt that is inside of them? How shall I tell my students who are poor to ignore the injustices of an imperfect and callous world and to learn despite the many wrongs of our society? What can I say that will make my students grow strong and make such gigantic contributions that even the most apathetic person will feel shame at having ignored their inalienable right to become first class citizens?

What can I tell my students who are poor of how much they are needed to discover a cure for cancer. . .to chart the course for others who trod the same fetid ways that they once knew? How can I teach my students to survive for the good of all humanity? How can I teach my students that to hate and to get revenge with our adversaries is to keep our own wounds green? What shall I say about the truths that have often been obscured and omitted? I now find that I have much to say to my students who are poor.

I will demonstrate by example that to be number one is to never look back at number two lest we trip and fall. I will tell my students the illustrious stories of the poor children of old and how with perseverance, stick-to-it-iveness, and yes, with a good teacher somewhere in between, these same poor men grew up to make some of the greatest contributions ever made in America. I shall take my students to the once-upon-a-time era when men, because of their poverty, burned the midnight oil while their fellow men slept in order to make sure that the setting sun in which they were born would one day rise and give off an illuminating light that would announce to the world that difficult does not mean impossible!

I will say to my students who are poor that if their lives are ever to be better they are the ones who will have to do it! Yes, I will tell my students that, if the ghetto is ever to become a part of past history, it is they, my students today, who must envision rebuilding tomorrow with the toil of their own backs and with the might of their own brains, and yes, of course, with the vision of a dream that they did not allow to die. None will do it for them. So this I will do for my students because I love them. My children who are poor must find the truth for themselves and pass that truth on to their children and to their children's children. In years to come, I believe that I will have armed my children with the ability to fish rather than having a fish given to them and that their children's children will venerate them, and then, of course, my love and guidance will not have been in vain.

For my students who are poor, it is education and the ability to lead themselves that will set them free.

21.
Into My Heart

I give might to the brain, determination to those who feel that they could never have made it without my help. . .I build all that is stalwart, long lasting and good. . .

I discourage being average. I believe that all of my students can learn if I do not teach them too thoroughly that they cannot learn.

I do not believe in "maybe," "might have been," or "we will see". . .I do not believe in tagging, labeling, Stanineing, ink-blotting and measuring until my students are left feeling illusive and low in self-esteem.

I do not believe that the kind of home a student comes from has anything to do with what that child can become. . .I do not make predictions without allowing my students to determine their own capabilities.

I refuse to let my students fail for they are yet too young to realize what is best for them. . .they are yet in the twilight of their years and therefore, failure has not left its whips and scorns on them.

Because I love them, I shall protect them from the hydra-headed monster called failure. . .knowing that their solace in the years to come will truly be the skills they have learned. . .these skills will never rust, tarnish, or go out of style. . .knowledge is forever.

I shall make my students comfortable with their locales. Yet with equal comfortableness they, too, can function as universal citizens of the world.

I will teach them to think for themselves so that they will not be girdled about in gusty winds like leaves blown from here to there believing whatever they are told.

I will learn to listen to their thoughts as well as get them to try to understand my own. I will earn their love so that they will respect me when it is time to chastise them. . .they then will understand that I love them all of the time, but I disagree with them some of the time. They, too, have the same opportunity to disagree with me. . .and to let me know that they, too, can teach me lessons of life.

I will not enunciate my hopes and express my principles for my students. I will not get more and more studies written rather than spend my time getting their lives right.

I will love them as I do my own children. I did not carry these children under my heart, but I will allow them to grow into my heart.

I cannot build enough bridges for all of them, but I will teach them to have the fortitude to build their own bridges. To take paths never taken and always leave a path for those who may follow.

I will attempt to teach them to be courageous enough not to run from everything that is difficult, but to face unflinchingly the problems of life and see them not as problems, but as challenges to living.

I shall encourage them to never rest on their past laurels. That good today does not mean forever. And to know that they will never be out of the stress of doing, achieving, pursuing. . .that excellence is a non-ending process, and that they will never arrive in the Land of the Done.

I will attempt to make my students curious and discontent for without the two there is no progress. I want always to say with pride: "Those are my students; of them I am proud, when cometh more?"

Like Romeo's Juliet, I would like to feel that when I am no longer on earth my students will become like stars that will light the world with excellence, with self-determination, with pride. . .and that they, too, will say: "Come with me, I will show you the way." I would like for them to say, "Your problems are my problems. . .you are my brother, and you are not heavy."

My work is ageless. . .my work is timeless. . .my influence never dies. . .never ends. . .because you, my students, carry on what I have begun.

22.
In Pursuit of Academic Excellence and Safety

The responsibility for recreating excellence in education lies with parents and educators. We must examine our priorities and our methods and then restructure an educational system that builds on the strengths of our students and democratic society.

There is an old axiom that says, "When one cannot get milk from a cow then one should try a bull." I have one very special axiom of my own: American educators are constantly trying to put a Band-Aid on a hemorrhage.

We have fed far too many American students on overdoses of illiteracy and heaping portions of lowered self-esteem, and yet still expect them to behave like first-class citizens in the classroom. And this despite the fact that they have been exposed to a second-class curriculum that now has all of us staggering under an illiteracy figure of 23 million illiterates and 35 million functional illiterates with two million illiterates being added to that figure each year. These figures are cited in the baleful report, *A Nation at Risk.*

Far too many American schools have attempted to mass-produce students the way we mass-produce products: teaching in many cases with the same callousness that factory workers turn out nuts and bolts. We have standardized classes for non-standardized students. We are so busy teaching students that two plus two makes four and that Paris is the capital of France, that we often fail to teach our students they are unique and special and moreover they must therefore not hurt others who are miracles also.

Socrates was right: "Straight thinking leads to right living." Our students have not been taught to think critically and analytically. They have been so busy drawing lines from here to there on xeroxed prepackaged lesson plans, which far too many teachers use, that they do not have one lofty thought. Is it any wonder, then, they are out to destroy the world and themselves in a bath of hate?

We have told our students how inferior they are through lowered test scores, lowered SAT scores, and school environments resembling incarceration centers where students have to line up in militaristic rows to use the bathroom, eat lunch, and to pass from class to class. The only apparent difference between some schools and penal institutions is that the students are allowed to go home in the evening!

We have made the curricula easier and easier and the banalities of these easy-to-teach, easy-to-read curricula create the hydra-headed monsters we see in our students. Educators refuse to accept responsibility for our students' failures and, therefore, we continue to head for a brick wall blindfolded. We have Stanined, ink-blotted, tested, and measured students until they feel that finding the real them is an elusive and almost impossible process.

Poor education is the topic of the day in our issue-a-week society right now. I suppose it is easier to blame the students than to take a hard look at the curricula and methodology used in our schools.

Students do not vote; they do not make the rules for our society; they do not elect our officials; and they have very little to say as to what happens to them. It seems to me that adults are focusing on getting the reasons for our students' behavior in schools written rather than get the lives of our students right.

We, as adults, must not forget what it was like to be students. We can remember how boring a sermon at church might have been or those classes that we couldn't wait to get out of. Yet, can't we also remember those teachers who inspired us, who motivated us, whose classes seemed all too short? Can't we all remember at least one teacher who taught for the love of teaching rather than for a paycheck? And can't we remember the Agnes in *David Copperfield* who was always pointing upwards for her charges? If our children are not what they should be, we must remember that we, as educators, are the Pygmalions that carved them in the first place. We must carve well, for when these students become adults, we can carve no more.

Perhaps some of our own violence is erupting in our students. It is all too seldom we say to a student: "You are too bright to waste your time," rather than responding with negative behavior ourselves. How many times have we been more interested in the right answers from a student than in getting the life of that student right? Perhaps we need to forget some of the theories we learned in teachers' college and learn to use the fiber and core of our hearts. Emerson was right: "Man is astounded by common sense." We need to forget some of the advice given us by the mandarins of education and the "experts." It was the experts who got us into this mess in the first place.

Most children begin school excited about the voyage of life, excited about learning. . .until somewhere, somehow, they are turned off like a light bulb, never to come on again. Our society seems to be filled with people who consciously or unconsciously have all of the answers all of the time and humanity none of the time.

Visit the average teachers' lounge and the volatile conversations are usually about how inferior the students are, and how misbehaved they are. Too seldom do we hear teachers excited about their students' progress, or how well their students are doing. The doomsday cries that permeate the ambience of the faculty room or lounge reflect the same kinds of attitudes we have taught our students. The result is that far too many students are "faking it" until they make it out of school, or dropping out of school to listen to a drummer that they can keep pace with.

Imagine for a moment the head of a great corporation telling his employees he does not expect very much of them because their backgrounds are just a bit too inferior in the first place to expect very much. This kind of defeatist attitude does not leave much room for self-esteem. Too often this happens in our classrooms. In contrast, if we tell students they were born to win; we believe in them, we refuse to let them fail; and we love them all the time, but will disagree with them some of the time, we then remove some of the reasons for rebellion. If we reprimand students by first placing our hand on their shoulders in a caring fashion, there is an unvoiced sense of caring, and the students are more apt to respond in a positive fashion. None of us like to be belittled in front of others; it diminishes our self-respect by saying to us "the accuser is okay and we aren't."

We must once again make schools miniature societies which teach students how to function in the real world. We must once again offer our children the skills and self-determination that will allow them to raise their families in dignity. We must accept responsibility for our actions and acknowledge when we are wrong. Together, parents and educators must recreate the magnificent dream started in 1776—the dream that we can all be more than what we are. The Puritan work ethic must once again be rekindled.

Violence will die unborn in our schools when we as parents and educators once again relight the flickering candles of excellence in America so our children may dare to know that joy awaits them; and so the classroom once again becomes the workshop that will allow our children to wave the unfurled banners of freedom: Schools will bear the flame that will help enlightened citizens solve the problems of their locales and with equal effectiveness the problems of the distant universe.

Once again we must create students who can hold dominion over themselves, their homes, and their communities: Citizens who can leash the lightning and plumb the ether. We must once again create students who can steel the will in pleasure or pain to do what must be done to continue to make America the preeminent nation that it can be. We must not let the issues of the present "Age of the Shrug" with its "so-what?-its-not-my-problem" attitude maroon those of us who are brave.

Together we must become the parents of progress, the source of creativity, the designers of opportunity and the sculptors of human destiny. We all have a stake in the American dream. Miseducation, in all of its vilest forms, will assure us we will nostalgically look back one day at the American dream while we suffer the American nightmare. There must be a lesson in this for all of us.

23.
Living Philosophy

Our reluctance to care about others is the antagonist for freedom in the drama of human life. Learning, caring and doing are never easy enterprises, nor are courage and truth easy taskmasters. Hopes enunciated and principles expressed are simply not enough. Men must act in the face of stark reality and have the ability to face life's problems without flinching. The huge world that girdles all of us about puts all kinds of questions and tests to us, not to mention the difficulty of living from day to day.

Those of us with special talents have a special duty. Daily we must summon our wills to do the unwilling, to meet the unchallenged, and to live each day with the deliberation that it just may be our last day on earth. Great men are those who see that spiritual force is greater than material force, and that good thoughts do indeed rule the world. These thoughts must be maximally productive for both self and for society. Courageous is he whose spirit retains in pleasure and in pain the command of reason and caring about what we ought to care about.

Helping others is still the holy fire that keeps our purposes warm and our intelligence aglow. The spirit of giving one's self to humanity is a rare and noble virtue. The still sad music of humanity need not be as cacophonous as it presently is.

We must, however, come out of our air-tight vacuum compartments and unlock our long-locked rusty hearts and realize that each man's failure diminished us. The true spirit of greatness has been captured by those who have managed to lose themselves in something bigger than themselves.

This period demands much of us. These are the times that will maroon the hesitant and inspire the brave. We must stand up and shout, "This is my time and my place in this time," and we must all seek that place. We all have the potential for great deeds and today emphatically demands deeds—human deeds. Our sensitivity must become deeper, our visions must become more well-honed to the physiognomy of pain, and, most importantly, we must develop a quality of mercy for those who may not dare to hope without our constant encouragement. We all have a capability to know the pain and glory of other people if we choose to do so. We must all begin to use the fiber and core of our hearts for more than beliefs. We must put those beliefs into execution. This is the real test of Christianity.

We all will commit a sin of omission if we do not utilize all the power that is within us to discontinue being isolated from world affairs. Giving to those who cannot help themselves will help to buttress up the fragile peace of this world. We can no longer afford to live an age of the shrug—a "So what, it's not my problem" attitude.

You and I are the heirs of all ages. We can no longer afford to overlook the uglier side of our inheritance. We must all help to eradicate the legacy of abuse, degradation, the inhumanity of men blinded by prejudice, ignorance and personal spleen. To those of us who care, this is a special legacy and a challenge to accept the uglier side of life as well as the beautiful, and to answer this challenge is indeed a privilege and a responsibility. Accept it, I ask you, today, without fear. When this occurs, all men of all races will learn to live together in peace.

The only way man can achieve his own happiness is to strive for the happiness of others. Brotherhood must cease to be a sentimental, mushy-mouth, hypoglycemic thing. We must begin to realize that the brotherhood of man exists as emphatically as does the fatherhood of God.

I extend to each of you today an invitation to utilize yourself as a force to become potent weapons to fight against the present anger of the world. The hopeless, because of each of us, can become freedom's citadels, the arm of democracy, the voice of true brotherhood for all men.

It is the responsibility of all great people to forge the keys that will stir ambition. To stimulate ideas and disarm anarchy we must all become sources of inspiration, the aid of aspiration, the forces of positive determination that will one day become the hope of the young and the joy of age. We must all become the parents of progress, the creator of culture, and the molders of destiny.

Because of those of us who care today, we can hope to eradicate the scars of poverty, the stripes of toil, the pains of hunger. Together we shall bear in triumph the wisdom of all ages by making today different so that others may dare to dream of a tomorrow.

24.
Breathing Life into a Stone

Act 2, Scene 1, of Shakespeare's play *All's Well that Ends Well*, has a line that has always been important to me as a teacher. That line from the play says, "I have never seen a medicine that's able to breathe life into a stone." I made a pledge as a beginning teacher to become that medicine that would breathe life into a stone.

I have selected to work with the "stones" of society. These are the children that society and the experts declare impossible to teach. These are the children that you read about in the statistics. You know. . .those who are just a bit too poor, too inferior, too little motivated to learn. Tell me what cannot be done and you will see the "cannot" become "can." As I tell my students, remove the "t" from "can't" and you have "can."

We use Ayn Rand's *The Fountainhead* as our Bible. Every child from age three on is taught that he must never succumb to being a second-hander in society. Each child is given the skills to become a creator in society. We teach each child to become self-motivated, self-propelled, and self-directed. We teach each child that we cannot distribute until we have first created. Each class is given money for every skill in which they succeed. These monies are used to purchase goods that we provide for them. Purchasing day is usually Fridays, and those children who have reached millionaire status get the opportunity to shop first. Those children who have not worked to their fullest capacity get the leftover gifts. Soon, all children become creators, for they find that second-handedness is never comfortable. Today, the 8th-grade algebra class all made 100 on their weekly tests.

Yes, it is possible to breathe life into a stone. I do it every day. I have done it for seventeen years. Try it, you will like it.

About Marva Collins

Marva Collins is a former Chicago public school teacher who founded Westside Preparatory School in 1975. She is widely known for her "basics" approach to teaching, which includes strong emphasis on phonics and basic computing skills and which also incorporates the teaching of classical literature. In 1980, she was nominated by President Ronald Reagan to serve as Secretary of Education, an offer she declined in favor of teaching at Westside Prep. In 1981, she was the subject of a feature-length motion picture, *The Marva Collins Story.*

Hampton Roads Publishing Company
publishes and distributes books on a variety of subjects,
including metaphysics, health, complementary medicine,
visionary fiction, and other related topics.

To order or receive a copy of our latest catalog, call toll-free,
(800) 766-8009, or send your name and address to:

Hampton Roads Publishing Company, Inc.
134 Burgess Lane
Charlottesville, VA 22902